SPEAKING

GOD'S

FREQUENCY:

ALIGNING WITH GOD TO UNLEASH TRANSFORMATION IN FAMILY, LIFE AND BUSINESS

BY JON FULLER

WITH CONTRIBUTIONS FROM: SHAWN BOLZ, PAUL YOUNG, BOB HASSON, JEREMY BUTROUS, KASEY FULLER AND MORE!

FOREWORD BY: SHAWN BOLZ

Publisher's Note:

Scripture quotations are taken from the King James Version (KJV) of the Holy Bible 1967 Edition of the Scofield Reference Study Bible.

ISBN - 9781733254809

ISBN 978-1-7332548-0-9

9 781733 254809 >

Cover design, layout: Hemant Lal

CONTENTS

FOREWORD BY SHAWN BOLZ

This book will change or fine-tune your perspective as a Christian about what is available to you and what you can experience through and in your life.

Perspective is one of the main foundation blocks that we use when we build toward changing ourselves, and then continue to build toward having an impact on the world around us. Building perspective, though, takes an intentional process.

Let me explain: I remember when I was first married, and our good friend who is a therapist was talking to us and explaining that we were going to have to form a new conflict model based on deliberate choices, or else we were doomed to repeat any dysfunction in how conflict was modeled to us when we were young. Both my wife and I had wonderful families who didn't do conflict very well. Mine were avoiders—I watched my father sidestep his negative emotions, and sometimes I even thought he was being spiritual by bottling them up. I became introverted with my own negative emotions, trying to work out by myself what should have been handled in conversation and relationships. It was a bad model that I didn't even know I was using until we had some breakdowns in our communication and I went into the cave of my mind and heart. The good thing is a little friendly Biblical truth and psychological perspective changed my processor. I gained an understanding of how to grow in perspective that was not natural for me.

I had to learn the tools of sharing each step of my inner journey with my wife even if I felt an offense or was affected by her instead of letting it bottle up. It took the time of building

4

through intentional conversation with my therapist friend to show me that I needed these new tools.

As Christians, we think all of the best things in life that God intended for us are the most natural, and they will be once we mature, but they don't start out that way. Communication with God is one of the main points in this book, and it's one of the greatest areas of human resistance and unbelief when most of us start out. It takes intentionality in our pursuit of faith to actually grow into the belief that God has something to say to us. It takes even more faith to lay down our normal agenda and believe that He will bring a result through our lives that our talents, skills, and personality can't do on their own—AKA a God result.

Jon's book is going to take you on an inner pilgrimage that will challenge your lack of perspective, the inherited tools that exist in your relationship of your inner life with God. I teach people how to connect to God by hearing His voice all around the world. I have found that most people don't think God is interacting with them very much, and yet the Biblical perspective that Jesus lays out of relationship with Him is ongoing communication through the Bible and the Spirit.

Ask yourself the following: Do you believe He talks to you? Often? Do you know how to interpret and apply what He is saying? Are you satisfied with your own inner spiritual fruit of your connection to the Holy Spirit?

These are all questions that we should have profound individual goals in so that we can not only grow into a thriving relationship with God, but also so that relationship can affect the world around us.

As you read this book, Jon is going to ask you a lot of questions at the end of each chapter, and I want to encourage you to take time to reset even if you have answers for them right away. Don't go with the first thing that comes to your heart or mind—dig deeper, because if you want a more transformative result in your own inner journey with God, you are going to have to allow that deeper process. You are powerful to lead your journey with God.

This book is a vital manual for individuals, groups, leaders and even whole churches to realize the potential of the transformative power of the nature of God through communicating with Him in real ways that have real fruit. I highly recommend it.

Shawn Bolz
Author, Podcast Host, TV Personality
Exploring the Prophetic Podcast
Through the Eyes of Love Book
Translating God TV show

Chapter One

WORDS ARE TRANSFORMATION TOOLS

"Whatever you're facing, God has given you an incredible tool that you can start to use right now to transform your life. Your life was not meant to be lived in struggle and frustration, and God has provided us an amazing access to transformation. If you are reading this, you already have that tool with you. Have you used it lately? When used correctly, it leads to life and flourishing; if misused, it leads to death and destruction. So what is this powerful tool?

Proverbs 18:21 says, "The tongue can bring death or life; those who love to talk will reap the consequences" (NLT). I think the Good News Translation of this verse brings the point home in a whole new way. It says, "What you say can preserve life or destroy it; so you must accept the consequences of your words. "

This tool that transforms us is our words. Our words can have really good consequences, or really bad ones.

I know, saying words are powerful to transform your life sounds too simple. I used to think the same thing, until I had an experience that changed and empowered me in my life forever. My life has so dramatically transformed that I can't stop talking about it! Rest assured, if you feel skeptical about this power, that is okay. I was there too. I just ask you remember Malachi 3:10, when God says, "...And thereby put me to the test, says the LORD of hosts, if I will not open the windows of heaven for you and pour down for you a blessing until there is no more need (ESV)." Have you tried to put God to the test by using His word, to release the abundance He has for you emotionally, relationally and financially? This is your invitation to do just that.

My Story

I want to start by taking you back to the moment that changed my mind about this issue years ago. It all started on an early Sunday morning. I was in the basement having some quiet time, praying and reading the Bible. I felt the Holy Spirit tell me to read Ezekiel 37. Nothing about this was abnormal— God often spoke to my heart about passages that would turn out to be meaningful to me. As I turned the pages, the song started playing in my mind: "Them bones, them bones, them dry bones." This song was way before my time, but I had always enjoyed hearing it as a kid. I could feel the excitement rise up in me, and my skin started to get goose bumps. I knew my Father was about to show me something and I needed to listen.

In this passage, Ezekiel has a prophetic vision to help him understand God's heart for Israel. I want to look at this passage together, starting with the first verse in the New Living Translation, to see the power of words in action!

"The Lord took hold of me, and I was carried away by the Spirit of the Lord to a valley filled with bones. He led me all around among the bones that covered the valley floor. They were scattered everywhere across the ground and were completely dried out."

Do you ever feel this? I know, at that time in my life, I did. There were things in my life that I felt were dead and decomposing. Things like relationships, financial situations, and dreams. It's not like they were sort of living, or somewhat okay, or about to die—they were totally dead and dried-out bones. Not only was there no hope, but the idea that there could be hope was also dead. Maybe there are things in your life that feel the same way.

Let's continue with verse 3:
"Then he asked me, "Son of man, can these bones become living people again?"
"O Sovereign Lord," I replied, "you alone know the answer to that."
Then he said to me, "Speak a prophetic message to these bones and say, 'Dry bones, listen to the word of the Lord! This is what the Sovereign Lord says: Look! I am going to put breath into you and make you live again! I will put flesh and muscles on you and cover you with skin. I will put breath into you, and you will come to life. Then you will know that I am the Lord.'"

Ezekiel spoke this message and the bones came together with flesh and breath and became a great army. The story continues in verse 11: "Then he said to me, "Son of man, these bones represent the people of Israel. They are saying, 'We have become old, dry bones—all hope is gone...'".

God was showing Ezekiel that even things that looked dead could live. This is metaphorical, of course, which makes it powerful for us to apply to our lives today. In what area do you need hope? In what area do you need God to create an army of help where you have only seen dry bones and death and hopelessness? The passage finishes with God saying Ezekiel's words would restore hope. Verse 14 says: "Then you

9

will know that I, the Lord, have spoken, and I have done what I said. Yes, the Lord has spoken!'"

I loved this passage, but on that particular Sunday when I was in the basement, something felt different about it. I felt something was missing. There was something more God had to say. I turned my heart to God, and I heard his prompting: "Go to Genesis." I was not sure why at first, but then I noticed Genesis 1:26 — "Let us make human beings in our image, to be like us" (NLV).

I thought about this for a moment. In the story of creation, God had just finished creating the world by speaking it into existence. Then, I realized that out of all creation, humans were the only thing made in the image of God. That means we were the only ones given the ability to create though our words. I knew words had power, but at this point, it was as if a veil was lifted from my eyes. Finally it clicked. Not only did I know it in my head, I felt it in my heart.

I could end my story there, and part of me wants to, because what happened next might be challenging for some people to understand. At the time, it challenged me to my very core! I heard the Father say to my spirit, "I want you to speak over your finances and tell them to double."

Overcoming the Inner Cynic

Honestly, I wish I had been filled with faith, but like many of us, sometimes I struggle to know "for sure" if God is saying something or if it is coming from my own mind. My first thought was (I admit) that speaking over my finances like that was not something God would tell me to do. I strongly believed that it was greedy to ask God for something like doubled finances. Not that I didn't need it. I knew I needed my finances to double to be in a good place and meet my family's needs, but I did not feel good about asking for that outright. I did not believe life was all, or even mostly, about money.

The second thought I had was about the "name it, and claim it" movement I grew up in. People involved in this belief system went around and spoke out loud that God wanted them to be rich and have big houses and fancy cars. They thought that God was their genie to give them what they wanted and all they had to do was keep speaking it. I didn't agree at all with that mentality. It felt like people were trying to use God and thinking God was theirs to be used. It felt very disrespectful.

That moment in the basement was a real moment of testing for me. I did not want to speak to my finances! It made me feel I was going to sound like a crazy or greedy person. But, as I thought, I wondered what would happen if I didn't. What would happen if God gave me this opportunity and I missed it? I wanted to obey, so I said it. I told my finances to double. But as the words came out of my mouth, I heard God speak, "Now tell your finances to triple."

I couldn't believe this. Maybe he asked me to tell them to double first, because if he had first asked me to tell them to triple, I would have said no, thinking it was definitely too greedy. I wondered if my heart was in the right place. If you had been there that day, hearing me tell my finances to triple, you probably would have been able to hear in my tone that I was not sure I meant it. I mumbled it like a child being forced to say sorry. I didn't say it because I meant it, I said it because I was afraid there would be consequences if I didn't.

This point was not hidden from God. I heard Him again: "Say it like you mean it." I was challenged even more. What did I believe? Did I believe? Could God actually be calling me to discover Him, the God of abundance, in my finances? I was way past my comfort zone, being stretched into territory I wasn't familiar with.

By the time I left the basement, I had spoken over my finances and commanded them to double, triple, grow, and it was all kinds of (what I thought at the time was) crazy. I can't say for sure I had bought into the idea. But, looking back, that moment was a springboard that put me on a journey to see God demonstrate the miraculous in my life.

Over the next year, I did see the power of those words in my life. My finances grew exponentially! They did double and triple. But more importantly, what also grew was my belief that my words were truly powerful tools God gave me, and that He wanted me to use them. I realized if they were powerful over my finances, they were powerful to help my family, too. This wasn't just about money, this was about my life. God used money because at that moment in time, I needed money to keep taking good care of my family. God cared about that, but there was so much more, He cared about all aspects of my life and wanted to breathe life into everything that I was a part of.

Just to clarify, I still do not believe in the "name it, claim it" movement. Neither God nor our words are magical genies or powers. We can't just sit and say, "I want a million dollars" and have it appear. (Obviously, or we all would do that and the results probably wouldn't be good for us). The key is that we need to use our words to align our lives and promises with what we know God has already spoken over us. We have to align it with His Word. What has God spoken over you? What has God told you about what He has in store for your life? What do you feel you are called to do? What is in the Bible that God has already promised that you are not seeing right now?

If we go back to Ezekiel, we see that Ezekiel did not see the bones and say, "I want them to live, that would make me feel good and powerful. I'll go out there and speak to them!" No, instead, God showed him the bones and what was possible, and told him what to speak so that God's words could be released on earth, which would bless Ezekiel and all of Israel in the way God wanted them to be blessed: with hope! His words were powerful because they aligned with something God had already spoken. His words were given to him, but God was the one behind them.

How Do You Know: Experience or Logic?

As I think about the start of my own story, there are two things I've realized that I think may be helpful to share. First, many people would say they "know" something is true in their logic. If you are like me, you probably know in your mind that the Bible says that words are powerful. But there is another kind of knowing that you get, not through your mind, but through your heart by having an experience.

If you are thinking, "Yeah, Jon, I know words are powerful, so what?" I would respond that it sounds like you have a logical knowing, not an experiential knowing. Do you *experience* the power of your words on a daily basis?

Knowing because of logic and knowing because of experience are two very different things. I can know all there is about how to fly a plane, but unless I have a lot of experience flying a plane, I am not a pilot. You sure are not going to want to fly in a plane I pilot if I don't have actual experience! My logic is not powerful enough alone to make me successful in life. When it comes to the power of our words, knowledge without experience is not very powerful. Could you imagine if someone said they loved their spouse logically, but did not pursue an experience of love with them? Sounds like that relationship is doomed for failure! But how often do we do this in our relationship with God?

I like the way Ingrid Bengis puts it. She says, "For me words are a form of action, capable of influencing change. Their articulation represents a complete, lived experience." Again, I want to ask: When did you last experience the power of your words aligning with God's words? I want to encourage you that even if you know they are powerful, God has more than logic for you. God wants you to "taste and see" they are powerful. Why? Because Psalm 34:8 says that as we experience God, that is how we know He is good.

The second thing I want to share is to remind us that speaking God's word is what God wants, and it is Biblical! This book is not "the gospel according to Jon Fuller." God Himself is the one who tells us our words are powerful. If we go back to Genesis 1:26, we hear that part of our identity is that we are made to be like God. We are not made to be Him, but we are living our best life when we are imitators of God. And God created our entire reality with His words.

We are called to co-create things with our words. In the beginning, we were given authority to rule and reign over the earth. God spoke and passed His creation and transforming power to us! After everything God created, He declared it was "good." We are also called to use our words to make things that are "good."

What does that look like? In the coming chapters, I will be sharing many examples from many different people about what this can look like practically. But for now, I will just say that it looks like the ability to speak life and truth into existence. It is speaking in alignment with God's good and perfect truth. It is our responsibility to take care of what God has given us. It's very clear in Genesis that He created life, and told mankind to recreate and govern. God made man in the garden to be like Him. He gave us the ability to create and gave us an imagination. God created animals, but left it up to Adam to use his imagination to name them.

Isn't that amazing? God wanted Adam to use his own words to define them. I believe this is a prototype of what God desires for our life. He has had a plan and purpose since the beginning of time for us, and He wants to be part of the process of building that life. At any point we can walk away from that path if we desire—that's the free will He has given us—but if we choose to align with his words, we can flourish. Using our words well is part of how we do that. We all have free will and a choice in the life we are co-creating with God. God gave it to us, but it is up to us to define it.

Words as Creation Tools

As creators, we need the right tools for what we are creating. In this book, we are focusing on the tool of words to create a powerful, transformed life. Have you ever been in the middle of a project and known deep down inside there had to be a better tool out there to help get you to your goal? In my line of work, it happens all the time. As a contractor, my main business revolves around building and remodeling houses. If anyone knows the importance of having the right tool, I do!

I remember recently a time we were trying to finish up a job. One of my crews was painting a rental house, but they didn't have a paint sprayer with them. They started painting the trim with a brush. The project, which would have taken maybe an hour with a sprayer, would now take days! It was not that painting the house with a paintbrush was not possible. It was possible. The problem was that it was not a powerful, productive or easy way to transform the house. It would waste a lot of time and money if we had to pay for the labor.

15

In this situation, I had the team rent a sprayer, and they were able to finish painting the whole house by the next day. The investment was a little more upfront to get the right tool, but the amount of hours it saved us as a company saved us hundreds of dollars.

Yet, having the right tools does not guarantee we become successful. Again, it comes back to experience and practice. I am well aware that there are people who could be given a paint sprayer and would still not get me a good result, because they would not know how to use it correctly. Practice is also a valuable kind of investment. We practice now so we can live in a future where a skill is easy. It is no different with words.

How much have you invested in using your words to create transformation? Over the years, I have met many people who speak something once or twice, and then give up. They go back to painting with a spiritual brush of waiting for God to do something because the "spiritual sprayer" of their words is more complicated or it takes more investment of time to learn. But I assure you, the investment of time upfront saves us so much! It saves us pain and frustration and feeling powerless for the rest of our lives.

Along the same lines, how often have you tried to create transformation in your life by some means other than the ones God has given you? How often have you tried to use "tools" like trying to be better or ignoring that the problem is there? We have to be willing to use tools, or they won't help us.

When I look back over my life I clearly see there were times I was not willing to use them. The enemy wants to co-create, too. He wants us to co-create us into his image, the image of someone who is ultimately powerless and focused on destruction, disempowerment and despair. Through my life, there has been a battle over my words. They have been a huge asset, or a huge liability.

I can be a pretty passionate person at times, and it is easy for me to have an opinion about things. To be passionate can be a wonderful gift, but it can also create a challenge, because when I am upset, I am passionately upset. In that passion, I can easily speak things that I regret, or that start me on a track to co-create with the enemy. This is something that I try to be aware of every day. Recently, I found myself having to backtrack and reject things I had previously said.

I want to share this with you, because I hope you will find it helpful, genuine and relatable. I was doing a lot of work for another company, a company that attracts a lot of customers that I wouldn't usually do work for, which challenged me. They seemed to be more demanding and rude than those of other companies I'm used to working for, and they were very, very hard to please. In my frustration, I got out of alignment with God's words. I got to a place where I was saying destructive things out loud and repeating them, if not daily, then weekly.

The fruit of what I said was bad. I had started to co-create with the enemy. I found myself hating my job and speaking very negatively. I was on a fast, downhill roll. What I love about the Holy Spirit is that He quickly brought to my attention what I was doing. I went back to what I knew, and started speaking over my clients and business. I said things like, "Thank you Father that you bring me great clients, ones that are a blessing to me and my company. Thank you for profitable jobs and clients." The atmosphere changed and I got totally blessed. I couldn't believe it—I even started to hear more amazing and positive feedback instead of demanding and displeased feedback.

Later that day, I pulled up to a job, and the owner of the house I was working on asked if I could talk. After the couple weeks I'd just had, with so much negativity, I was thinking, "Oh crap, now what?" But the husband went on to say how impressed he was with the progress and how well I ran my jobs and crew. He said he went on my Facebook page and looked at our work and reviews. To be honest, even then I was thinking, "Great, I wonder what negative stuff he read?" Instead, he said how impressed he was with our work and that we have such great reviews. I was so encouraged and transformed by that moment. Your words can make all the difference in the direction of your day!

This brings me back around to the verse we started with. Proverbs 18:21 says, "The tongue can bring death or life; those who love to talk will reap the consequences." (NLT) This scripture is one of my all-time favorite verses. It resonates so much with me because in many ways, it sums up many big parts of my story.

A Spanish proverb says, "A word from the mouth is like a stone from a sling." A stone has the ability to destroy something bad, or also destroy something good, depending on how we choose to use it. I can use my words to destroy mountains that are hindering me and things that are holding me back. I can also use them to destroy the good in my own life. I encourage you to use your stones wisely to build the life you want and destroy the giants in front of you as God intended.

Part of knowing how to use our words correctly is to recognize the areas where we struggle to speak life. In these areas we have to check in regularly with ourselves. I wonder what those areas are for you? For me, I have struggled to speak life over my finances. I need to be vigilant over this area the most, because this is where the enemy would love to co-create death and ruin if I do not stay aligned with God.

I run multiple companies and have many projects going, and money can come and go really quickly at times. I feel great when I have money in the bank, and it gives me a sense of accomplishment. But the next day, or even hour, it can be one-tenth of what was there. At that point, I find myself emotionally down and speaking negative things over myself and my company.

The amazing thing is that I have grown so much in my ability to speak life. You can do this too! We have to practice to see the reward. As I have grown, I have seen the difference in my finances. My financial state is now more aligned with stability and God's will because of it.

There are many times I want to just say what I'm thinking, but a friend once told me that we all have to work to make our words sweet, because we end up eating them someday. I had to learn this lesson the hard way. I have spent many years speaking and feeding myself on poisonous, rotting words, and have gotten emotionally or spiritually sick off them. Like vomit, it felt like a relief to get it out, but when it came time to eat the fruit of my words later...well, no one wants to eat something that is like vomit!

We have been given the ability and privilege to speak whatever we want in private. In the USA, we have also been given freedom of speech in public life. We can freely say what we want, but that doesn't mean there aren't consequences. Scripture says we will be judged by every word that proceeds out of our mouth (Matthew 12:36).

I have heard it said that people speak an average of sixteen thousand words a day. If the average life span is 78.7

19

years for Americans, we have a lot of words to use for good or evil. Let's think of it like this: in life, you'll have around 459,608,000 words to use. Each of these words has power to direct your life. Each word can influence your circumstances. Once we use a word, we can never, ever get it back or reuse it, and we will have to give an account of it to God.

I know, it is not as easy as it sounds. Words are powerful, but they will not be powerful to transform your life unless you know how to use them, and you are not simultaneously using them for destruction. Before we close this chapter, I want to point out one other thing about how we must use our words to be effective and see the transformation God has for us.

In the basement that day, when I was so changed, I realized that words are essential. But, if you remember, God encouraged me to speak like I meant it. Why? Because behind the words, at a deeper level, I needed a heart change. I needed to be able to think about my finances like God did, so I could speak over my finances like God did. The second half of Luke 6:45 says, "What you say flows from what is in your heart." (NLT)

Many people do not guard their hearts. At times, I have not done that well. At times, I ended up partnering with the enemy and speaking death. Sometimes we do this because we are simply frustrated that God does not take over our life completely and make it happen. Maybe we do not know we are responsible for partnering with God. But, whether we like it or not, He will not make our decisions for us! Sometimes we read about the plan God has for us, but when we do not see it work out in our timeframe, our words start to poison the good God is trying to bring.

We should be careful not to passively accept whatever comes into our life and think it is God. God has a good plan for our lives. The Bible clearly says, "God causes everything to work together for the good of those who love God and are called according to his purpose for them." (Romans 8:28) He can work all things to His glory for those who love Him and serve Him. It doesn't matter where you have come from or what you are struggling with. We always get the choice to come alongside God and speak His will and goodness into our lives. Or, we can speak the words of the destroyer. We just can't then blame God when we start to feel powerless and like our life is falling apart. We were the ones that spoke those things, not God. Life, for humans, is not about being bossed around by God. It is about partnership and co-creation. Even if we go back to the Garden of Eden, God created animals, but wanted Adam to partner by creating names for them.

This process is not as easy as it sounds. Speaking life takes work and practice. Speaking life means we have to accept that the impact is not always immediate, and does not always happen in the ways we anticipate. Sometimes, the change that our words create is not in the external world, but in the internal world, where they bring light and hope to us, which then empowers us to keep going. I want to encourage you that your words don't work like a microwave. In the basement, in order to speak God's words, my heart had to change. So, there is work we have to do in our hearts in order to see our words have the power of transformation and the power to bring good like God intends us to have. The reason I wrote this book is to share what I have learned to help you get from knowing that words can be powerful, to seeing that power daily in your life. In the next chapter, I want to share what I have learned about another tool that is a co-creator along with our words: love. Our words are heard and seen, but our love is felt and unseen, and if these two things are not working together, we will not have much success in seeing our words transform our world.

Transforming Steps:

I want this book to be an experience for you as well, not just words. I hope you will consider these next steps, so this chapter can be a catalyst for real, powerful change. No matter where you are starting from, and what you have been though, you can start today to speak God's words and see the transformation in your life.

1. Spend some time talking to God and others about an area of life where you struggle to speak God's will and life. What is your area of weakness and vulnerability when it comes to your words? Maybe, like me, it is in finances, or maybe it is in relationships. Maybe it is in self-esteem or in how you speak about yourself. Try to identify this for yourself.
2. Identify one area where your words are strong and you feel confident that you often get it right and speak God's words. It may be that you are better at speaking life over others than yourself. Or speaking about a talent or skill you are good at, and seeing that grow.
3. Find a partner to help you in this journey. Ecclesiastes 4: 9-10 says, "Two people are better off than one, for they can help each other succeed. If one person falls, the other can reach out and help. But someone who falls alone is in real trouble." My wife has been such a huge blessing to me, because she catches me when I am starting to align with the enemy in the way I talk. She helps remind me the value of spending my limited amount of words wisely. This partner does not have to be a spouse, but it should be someone you can trust to give you honest feedback about the words you are speaking. Ask them if your words usually bring life, or destruction.

Chapter Two

THE TRANSFORMING POWER OF LOVE

"Words are powerful, but behind every word God speaks, there is a more powerful force of love. In some ways, His words are the tangible example of His heart, and words are the expression of our heart as well. Luke 6:45 says, "What you say flows from what is in your heart." Proverbs 4:23 says, "Guard your heart above all else, for it determines the course of your life." So in order to be able to see our words transform our lives in positive ways, we have to have our hearts right.

God's love is the most powerful thing in the world. It created us and is also the motivation behind His words, which continue to transform and create us into his likeness. On our journey with God, if we do not understand this power, we will get stuck. I don't say this from the perspective of someone who grew up feeling loved, or understood, or having it all figured out—quite the opposite.

Growing up, my mom was in and out of prison, and my dad was what I call a "white-collar drug addict." I never in my life felt secure. I never understood being loved by family. My dad's family made comments about me not being true blood family because my dad is not my biological father (though that became more of a focus later in my life). Things were said that really hurt me, and I can genuinely say I have never done anything but just love my family, love them for who they are and long for them to love me back. When it comes to the place in my heart where love should be, I guess you could say I had a lot of hurt and insecurity. I had a relationship with my family, but it still never felt like I fully belonged. To make matters worse, when I was nine years old, my three-year-old brother died, and that set our family in a downward spiral.

My point is, I didn't grow up in an environment that helped me feel loved. But God's love has transformed me through the words He has spoken to me and the experiences He has given me. His love is not only about loving us unconditionally and stopping there, but is meant to fill each and every place of insecurity and hurt, to cover them in love so they disappear!

Breaking Down the Walls to Encounter Love
Recently, I was sitting in the living room with my wife and kids. It was Sunday, so we decided to do some worship together and prophetically speak and pray over each other. Now, please don't get spooked when I say "prophesy." Prophesy is simply speaking the words of God in love. You probably do this all the time, regardless of what you call it. The Bible says in 1 Corinthians 14:3, "But one who prophesies strengthens others, encourages them, and comforts them." We were not doing anything other than that. So, on that day, we all had a turn sitting in the middle to be prayed for, and the moment I sat down, a song came on and the lyrics said: "He is jealous for me, He loves like a hurricane" and the moment I hear He is jealous for me, I can hear the Father say in my spirit, "I am jealous over you, Jon, I guard you, I love you, I am so jealous of our relationship that I would never allow anybody to intervene in that love."

Some might have been thrilled to hear this, but for me, I had put up a wall in my life because I've been hurt so many times, so deeply, by people close to me, that I don't allow them to love me. It is not that I don't love, but I never truly connected on that deep level. So, I was having this moment with God and questioning if I was really hearing him, or making it up. And I heard the Lord say, "I saved this song to come on for you while Kasey prayed over you," and then Kasey laid hands on me and started praying and she just started weeping and she said, "God just wants you to know that He loves you, and that He is so madly in love and that He is playing this song for you."

Well, God knew I needed confirmation to believe, and that was confirmation, and I just started weeping. Kasey went on to say prophetically, the Lord just wanted me to know that the hurt from my family, the withholding of love, the lack of interest or care never came from Him, it wasn't Him. Kasey felt God kept on saying that He saw the hurt and that He never intended that for me, and He was hurt by seeing people with free will hurt me, and that it wasn't His fault, He did not do that , but because He was not a controlling God, He allowed others to have free will, and that He wanted me to know that.

It was a powerful moment, but it didn't end there. Later that day, I watched the movie *The BFG* with my daughter, and the story goes that there is this little girl who was an orphan and she was raised in an orphanage and she goes out to the giant land and goes before the queen and the queen brings her into her home to be part of royalty. The moment she's coming into the palace, I heard the Holy Spirit say, "You've been an orphan your entire life. When are you going to step into royalty and whom I've called you to be?"

I broke. My walls broke right down, and I was just weeping and crying, and I didn't want my daughter to see because I didn't want to ruin the movie. I felt so overwhelmed by the love of God. I always wanted to belong, and it felt like

He was extending that to me and more, to be in a place to rule, and I could feel how much He desired to infiltrate the walls around my heart and restore it. To be honest, its painful, and it hurts, and it feels like a breaking is going on in the walls that I relied on to keep me safe as a child and young adult.

It's not that I don't love as a father, and not that I don't know that I am loved, but there's a difference between knowing that you're loved and allowing yourself to be loved, and allowing yourself to step into royalty. I've truly have never done that—it's a process, its painful, it hurts. I am still trying to work through everything that happened that day and receive the power of what He is doing. So I just want to say that I know it is easy to encourage you to go for it, but I also know that when we do aim to align our hearts with God and love, often there is some pain that gets in the way that needs healing. It may feel like God is breaking down everything about us and who we are, but I assure you, He does it to build us back up.

For years, I have known that I am loved in my mind, but as I said in the last chapter, there is a difference between knowing and experiencing or feeling it in a heartfelt connection kind of way. This is what the Father wants to do, not just with me, but with you, and with everybody. I share this to share that this is the power of transformative love. In John 14:18, Jesus says, "I will not leave you as orphans; I will come to you." (ESV).

I am so thankful for a God that does not leave us as orphans. No matter where we came from, or what we have been through, His love can reach us, transform us, and cover "a multitude of sins" and disconnections and pains that we have experienced from others. His love is enough to make up for what was done to us on purpose or by accident, to transform us to be the best version of ourselves, without lack, without living with the constant infection of pain and

26

orphanhood. 2 Timothy 2:12 says, "If we endure, we will also reign with him." This is our destiny!

In my own life, the last six months has been the most overwhelming presence that I've felt of God in years. I can just be driving down the road and I'll listen to the words of a song and I'll feel the presence of the Father so heavy and so strong, almost as if He is singing certain parts of the song over me. And if I just think about it, I literally almost start to cry because of His goodness. The tears are a cleansing experience. God is with me, acknowledging my pain and creating a solution for my future.

The Extreme Love of God

Through the years, I've heard that I was so loved that Jesus gave His life for me at the cross, and died for me. I don't know about you, but sometimes it seems like this can become a cliché saying. We get used to hearing it, but don't know how to let that knowledge transform us. God did not just love us so much He sent Jesus to die. He loved us so much that He wanted to create us in the first place! God was fine without us. It is not like He needed us to help Him, or be something for Him. The only purpose for which we were created, then, was love! In the story of creation, the Father took dust from the ground and formed it in His hand and molded man together. Our Father breathed life into man.

What God did was He gave of Himself; He gave of His time and of His physical being. He gave of Himself, and if we believe the scriptures that "God is love," then, in that exchange, He gave us love. As we read the account, He also spoke everything else into existence, but it was man that He stopped and made with His hand. It was our first example, I believe, of love. God did not need us, but He chose us. He had angels and other heavenly beings, but yet He still chose to hand-make us. Love was the motivation that drove His creation. Love was the motivation behind His creation of us, and if love can create something out of nothing, why can it not also transform what already exists?

The amazing thing is that God is love, and in 1 Corinthians 13, Paul sums up not just a passive love, but shows us how love looks, how we experience love and how we identify what love is. I believe when we do anything in contrast to God's definition, then it is not from Him. I don't believe anything good can be done if it's not done in love. Here are the first six verses for inspiration:

"If I speak in the tongues of men and of angels, but have not love, I am a noisy gong or a clanging cymbal. And if I have prophetic powers, and understand all mysteries and all knowledge, and if I have all faith, so as to remove mountains, but have not love, I am nothing. If I give away all I have, and if I deliver up my body to be burned, but have not love, I gain nothing. Love is patient and kind; love does not envy or boast; it is not arrogant or rude. It does not insist on its own way; it is not irritable or resentful; it does not rejoice at wrongdoing, but rejoices with the truth. Love bears all things, believes all things, hopes all things, endures all things."

These verses tell us that we are loved with an extreme love. It NEVER gives up; it endures despite anything. We are not just loved with a passive, cliché, greeting-card-love. We are madly loved by God Himself! God is constantly pursuing us. I can't help but think of the demonstration of His love through Jesus's teachings in the New Testament. Jesus says, "What do you think? If a man has a hundred sheep, and one of them has gone astray, does he not leave the ninety-nine on the mountains and go in search of the one that went astray?" (Matthew 18:12). Jesus tells us this is what the Father is like. He will leave all others and pursue you. I think of the prodigal son, who blew it big time and, yet, Father God still opened

28

his arms wide and forgave! We don't deserve it, but yet he pursues us. It's an unrelenting love; it is always waiting for us to invite Him into our lives.

I love the story of the one sheep, because it ties in to the reality that we are all God's favorite. We actually need to know that to operate at our best! And I don't say that to make you feel good. In fact, I used to think this idea was ridiculous. But a few years ago, that all changed. I was in a church parking lot and I was part of the prophetic team. The format was that there was a teaching, and then everyone would practice prophesying over each other. When I was in the parking lot, I heard God say, "You're my favorite," and I remember shrugging it off. I thought, "Whatever, this is weird, how can I be God's favorite?" I didn't quite understand it, but I could feel the presence of God so strong, and so heavy. I had tears in my eyes, it was so powerful.

So we went inside and a man was standing by the door and he looked at me, and all he said was, "I just keep hearing that God wants you to know that you are His favorite." He just kept on saying it over and over, even as I was initially resistant. It was like, God was definitely trying to make a point! God was pushing Himself into my space, pursuing me with unrelenting love. He was letting me know He loved me and I was His favorite.

The man then told me all the things that He felt God was saying He loved about me, and then again He was just like, "You are God's favorite, you are His favorite." It was so powerful, because it just changed my whole perspective. All of a sudden, I thought, "Well, maybe I am God's favorite, maybe He does really love me and He will push through my walls to tell me." I think these kind of moments allow us to break anger off and so many things that are inside of us. Things in our hearts that are barriers to living in and then speaking in love. The moments also change our personal filters of how we see people. That instance allowed me to know how the Father felt about me, which allowed me to move past who I thought I was.

God has enough time and resources to prove to us that we are His favorite. People in our lives may have a "favorite," and that person gets the bulk of their time, love, energy, gifts or understanding. But God's resources are unlimited ,and He is so unlike man that we can all be His favorite and have all we need.

Fear of Punishment and the Blessing of Obedience
What does this change how we experience God and His love for us? I believe I am able to see God for who He is and not who I thought He was. I always thought I saw Him as a God I had to please and serve, like He was a task master, and when I didn't do something right He was angry and ready to punish me for my bad deeds.

That understanding was so wrong, but I have had to change my heart and mindset. I couldn't see Him for whom He was but rather for whom I had made Him out to be. Seeing God for whom He is has allowed me to work through my mistake and see He was always trying to lead me down the right path because He loved me. He was always there, trying to champion me into the greatness He created me to be. God has always been trying to restore His people back to their original design of what He intended.

I even saw the ten commandments at this time as totally different; I believed they weren't just rules that He had set into place and He was sitting there waiting for me to break them so He could punish me, but also that these laws were set into motion to protect relationships, and when people broke them toward me, it hurt me, and He did not want that.

In 1 John 4:18, He says that if we fear, it is because we are not aware how loved we are. Also, that fear has to do with punishment. I was unable to accept love, at times, because I feared punishment.

But obedience is so much more than just rules. When God asked for obedience in the old testament, he was trying to keep His children safe. When he tells me things, He does so to keep me safe, to keep me from hurting other people and hurting myself. When we see God from a place of how He loves us, it allows us to see what His Word really means, and the heart behind it. We are able to become who He says we are; we are able to let go of the regrets and the shame and the hurt that we carry. So as we allow His love, it's almost like there is an emptying of sin, of negativity and of hurt, of anger and all those things.

We are so loved, but most of us have never experienced love like that. I've been on this quest with God, thinking about how He can love me that much, and why. There's a Jesus Culture song that says, "Your love is fierce." That is the love of God that transforms! His love is not a thought, and if we accept His love on a heart level, we cannot help but be transformed. His unrelenting pursuit of love is a constant, wave after wave after wave. Have you ever experienced so much of the love of God that you think you just can't take it anymore? That is our destiny, and that is our calling as children of God.

I would say that many problems in our families and culture are due to the fact that we are not sure we are loved. God is love. So, without God, we are without the source of love, and that makes life harder. One of my favorite verses in Mark 6:34 says, "When he went ashore he saw a great crowd, and he had compassion on them, because they were like sheep without a shepherd. And he began to teach them many things."

I can relate to that feeling. For parts of my life, I felt like a sheep without a shepherd. But in this verse, Jesus steps out of the boat and He sees a huge crowd and He shows, not judgment, but compassion. In this scripture, He shows His love toward us as a human race. We're just completely lost without His love and direction, and even when we don't recognize that we need Him or what's going on, He literally steps out and takes time because of His love for us. He wants to teach us the right way; He desires us to live abundantly because that is how he created us to live—in love and abundance!

The hardest part is allowing His love into our lives and giving it a place to speak into us. When we allow the Father's love to penetrate us like He originally intended, it allows us to be transformed into the image of that love. As we allow His love into our lives it allow us to love purely. And here is the point: that love, and that feeling of being a favorite, creates a transformation.

His unconditional love allows us to recognize our faults and be okay with them. We know that we are loved, no matter what, and it enables us to have a process of working through them. If we know that we are loved, I think first and foremost it allows us to look at faults and forgive ourselves and move on. It allows us to operate to from a place of whom God sees us as and not whom we currently are. And I love that, because I think when God speaks over us and sees us, sometimes He's speaking over us of whom we are, but not whom we recognize ourselves to be. That's hard sometimes, because we know we're broken or we see ourselves broken, and we sit in that, and when God tells us whom we are and we step into that, it gives us freedom! Not only freedom, but being on the process and the journey of that, I think, gives us the freedom to be ourselves and not allow fear or failure to overwhelm us.

I believe this allows us to get beyond ourselves and see what we can contribute to others with what God has given us. We can only give what we have. If I am made in God's image and I don't allow all that He is to flow through me, then I am operating from a place of brokenness. God's love allows me to be made whole. God designed us on purpose, for a purpose. And if we step out into what God has for us, without being whole, we are operating in a deficit. God's love makes us complete and allows us to step into all that He has for us.

I think we have these encounters and these moments in our lives when God shows up because we want Him to. We invite Him into our space and allow Him to co-create with us what our life can be like. When we do, it is life-changing and altering. It is like He's going through the old files on the hard drive of our heart, sweeping them to clean out the files that have bad information or pain, and adding files of love and acceptance.

So, how are we transformed by the experience of love? God is outside of time, and the amazing thing is that a transformation with God can take no more than a moment. He does not need the time we might think it takes in the natural world. His love can completely take us off the grid of what we thought was possible for us. I think everything that God does is out of a place of love, because that is whom He is. God doesn't just love us; He is the source of where love comes from. What amazes me is that, as we spent time with Him, the overflow and presence of whom He is rest on us. I know when I spend time with the Lord and I feel like I really press in, I can literally feel His presence, and His love and comfort surround me like a blanket. I become a different person, I live a different way, I think a different way, I speak a different way.

Partnering With God's Transformation

To truly be transformed, sometimes we need to ask. We don't know how people feel unless we ask. There are times people will tell us things, like how they feel about us, but they don't usually say it or just come out directly with it. It is usually done in an environment that has been cultivated and nurtured, and I feel like it's the same with the Lord. I know it can be a weird thought for a lot of people to even ask this, but if we don't ask the Father how He feels about us, how are we going to know? We literally need to spend time with Him in a quiet place and just ask Him, "How do you feel about me?" instead of thinking we know already. James 4:2 says, "You desire but do not have, so you kill. You covet but you cannot get what you want, so you quarrel and fight. You do not have because you do not ask God." (NIV) If you do not ask God how he feels about you, you will feel a need to quarrel and fight and struggle to get love in the world. But God invites you simply to ask Him!

How else might I encounter God's love? One thing I've done over the years is read and reread my journal. I grab my journal and I just start writing—sometimes things just start to flow out and other times I have to make myself, but I always start from a place of thanksgiving and just thanking the Lord for His goodness and His love toward me, especially if I do not feel it at that moment. We don't feel like writing those things, but if we just write it out, things just start flowing, or at least they do for me. That is one thing that I've done for years to help me. A thankful heart is a much better place to live a life from than anger and bitterness.

Love can transform us, and we can use it to transform others! But the danger is that the way we use words is one of the primary ways to share love or to share something other than love. I haven't always got this right, and it has taken many mistakes to start to learn about this the hard way. I think we typically speak how we feel, or at least I do. And for years, I've allowed my emotions and how I felt about myself to come out recklessly, creating an environment where negativity, hurt and anger breed and grow.

So, I would like to go back to where we started this chapter. According to God's word, whatever is in your heart is what you will end up speaking. But when we step into God's love and allow Him to transform us and love us, our words naturally begin to change. When we allow Him to heal our wounds and realize we are his favorite, our thought process begins to change; then, once our thoughts change, our words begin to change, and our actions change as well. When we begin to speak from a place of freedom and being loved, it alters the atmosphere around us. My freedom begins to create freedom around me, because it's the overflow of whom I've now become.

For me, Luke 6:45 is like the check-engine light in my car. What are your words revealing about your heart? Is your heart filled with faith, hope and love? If it is not, you cannot expect to just speak things and see the transformation you want in your life. You have to have a heart and mind aligned to God. If you feel you are not there, I get it! I wanted to share my journey in this chapter because I wanted to be real and authentic. I am not fully there, much less always there. Not at all, but what I do know is that as you and I continue to purposefully and intentionally invite the experience of God's love into our lives, our hearts are transformed. Think of it like any other relationship—when you are looking to start a relationship, you have to be intentional about inviting the other person to do things, going out of your way to connect and be attentive and intentional. It is the same with how we need to pursue our relationship with God.

As we pursue this relationship, we will find that our words will automatically become more powerful to transform our own life. They will be more powerful because we will be speaking in alignment with love, with God's heart and with truth. Even as I write this, though, I know that some of us really struggle to know how God speaks, and we feel that connection is not as strong as it could be. Sometimes the idea of "hearing" from God feels vague. In the next few chapters, I have asked some of my friends to contribute their thoughts about how they hear from God to show you the many ways God speaks and to be excited and empowered to feel connected and hear His words in new ways for yourself.

In this chapter, we have talked about God's love. But how do we hear and experience God's love and access the power it has when we need it? In the next chapter, I am excited to share with you contributions from others who have a track record of hearing this way from God. This chapter includes thoughts from Shawn Bolz, Paul Young, Bob Hasson, Jeremy Butrous and Kasey Fuller, and if that is not enough, at the end of this book, I have included contributions from more people like Danny Silk, Brian Head Welch, Seth Dahl, Ambassador Dr. Clyde Rivers, Ryan LaStrange and Brad McClendon! I have asked them to share with you what they hear, how they hear it, and how it changes them. I hope this will give you direction and excitement about hearing the words God wants to speak directly and specially to you in your daily life so that you can align your words with His and start transforming.

Transforming Steps:

1. When did you most feel God's love? How did you feel it? How did it transform you?

2. Do you feel God is a punisher, trying to control, catch or criticize you? If so, consider where these thoughts and feelings come from? Read scriptures about God's love and compassion to remind you of the truth.
3. What are your recent words revealing about where your heart is at?

Chapter Three

HOW TO HEAR GOD'S TRANSFORMATION PLAN FOR YOUR LIFE

"One of the biggest questions I get from people when I share this message is about how to *hear* from God and know what He is saying. My transformation started because I "felt" God speak to me, and then it was confirmed through His word. But how do we "feel" what God is? How do we "hear" Him speak?

I have spent three years interviewing and getting to know the amazing stories of God speaking, on my podcast, *Are You Real*. Now, I want to let you in on the experience of how God speaks, and to hear some of the amazing experiences of others to encourage and inspire you! I don't want you to think that the way I hear God is the way people are "supposed" to hear God. Nothing could be farther from the truth! Over the years of recording my podcast, I have discovered how impactful it is to hear the words and stories of others, and when I do, I am released into greater levels of faith and even the ability to acquire a new "language," or way of hearing God, that I never knew existed! I want this for you.

There are many ways to hear God, and they are usually very personal. The writings that follow are just a few examples, and I hope you are encouraged and inspired by these stories to move into greater things that God has for you.

The first contribution I want to share with you is from my friend Shawn Bolz. Shawn is the author of *Translating God and Modern Prophets*, and he has a long track record of hearing God in specific and accurate ways. Here is what Shawn has to say about hearing God's word and how it helps us be an agent of change and transformation in the world:

You Have the Mind of Christ
SHAWN BOLZ

I grew up in a Christian family that led me to believe a relationship with God is interactive. But even with that knowledge, it took years to believe that God was speaking to me. Even after some of the most amazing once-in-a-lifetime encounters, they sometimes felt more like a dream afterward. I had the opportunity to talk myself out of them, but I just dared to believe them, and the fruit was so outrageous that I dared over and over.

I hear God mostly through impressions or hearing His voice inside my spirit. I also get a lot of symbolic mental pictures. My life has been marked with several open visions, and I have heard the audible voice of God on a few occasions. My most notable encounter felt very "face-to-face." I have grown so much in my relationship with God as I have learned to hear His voice clearly. This was an intentional process for me. I grew up around a lot of people who were world-renowned for their ability to hear from God, and it made me believe that it was possible, but I felt distant from the ability to consistently hear Him. I opened the Bible one day to Matthew 5:4 and read, "What delight comes to you when you wait upon the Lord! For you will find what you long for." This changed my mind. I just knew that I wouldn't even be aware of this desire if it wasn't for God wanting to give me faith for it, so I practiced and stopped spending religious time with God and really drew myself into a relationship with Him. It was hard, because I even began to practice hearing from God for others, and thus began a ten-year journey that made me love and hate this pursuit all in one package.

Thank God it has become much easier for me to hear God over the years as I practice. It is really amazing once you know yourself how much more you can know God. 1 Corinthians 2:16 says that we have the mind of Christ. I feel most of the ways that He speaks are through sharing His thoughts and perspectives with us, but if we don't know who we are or if we don't know what we want, then it is hard to distinguish between God's and our thoughts. I have gone on a deep journey of learning how to love myself and love others the way God does. I have gone on an identity journey that has lasted decades, but the fruit of it is that I usually can really distinguish God's thoughts from my thoughts.

I feel like now I am aware of doing life with God's Spirit. Just like I make my wife aware of my heart, decisions, and process—sometimes she just listens but other times she interacts with me. Sometimes she interacts to bring direction, other times to bring affirmation. Sometimes she even challenges what I am thinking. My relationship with God for me is like this; I include Him and know He can talk at any point. I am surprised when He does but almost equally surprised when He is silent for a time.

My most treasured experience was all about God's love. I could feel His heart beating for each of the billions of souls on the Earth and for everyone who would ever be born. I then saw whom I was supposed to love, which became the sense of calling and purpose I have now. It was several people groups and within an industry. It was very surreal and changed the way I pray and how I feel just called to some people like they are my tribe. Because of that, I feel an instant chemistry, love, and affection, and I see them for whom they are. For over a decade, I have never been "rejected" but always welcomed into places where my tribe is. I have been about to counsel, advise, and have vulnerability with people outside of the Church, but it didn't come because I was going to change the world or because I felt a missional purpose to spread God's word. It came because I felt His love through this encounter and have been able to be driven by this passion since then. I know it can come across sounding hokey, but my destiny, all growing up, was also the mission or purpose I felt called to. It was not some abstract destiny forced on me that felt awkward and unrelatable. My destiny was what was already in me to do! After this encounter, my destiny was the people I get to love, and my calling was the toolset God has given me to get to them and help them. This has put me in Presidents' offices, celebrities' homes, and multinational company chairmen's dinners, but also has brought me to war zones, dumps in third-world countries, and red-light districts, among some of the most forgotten and abused people.

I have some amazing stories of how God's words transformed me and others because I really believe God is amazing. One of my favorites involves politics. I actually heard God about who He wanted to pick as the president of South Korea three terms ago. I heard many very private things that were in the man's heart, about why God wanted to use him as a President and what he had been praying about. I had the opportunity to meet with him while he was campaigning, and it was a tipping point for him. I ended up going back to South Korea several times while he was running and sharing the perspective God gave me about him to many influential people, and the tide turned for him. I remember him sending me a letter that said, "Thanks for believing in me and helping me win the election," and it was signed by him. Wow! I have many of these stories now, but my occupation is centered around inspiring people to hear from God, so I get to hear the greatest stories from them as well.

For more information on Shawn Bolz, check out www. bolzministries.com.

Shawn is an author, a TV host (see him on season four of *Dreams & Mysteries* on Daystar!), a spiritual advisor, a producer, and a minister. He is passionate about seeing individuals and groups learn how to be the most connected, best versions of themselves through their relationship with God. His focus on having a genuine relationship with God, creativity through entertainment, and social justice has brought him around the world to meet with churches, CEOs, entertainers, and world leaders. He is the author of several books including *Translating God, God Secrets, Modern Prophets*, and *Exploring the Prophetic*. Shawn Bolz is also the founding pastor of Expression58 Christian Ministries, a ministry focused on the entertainment industry and the poor in Los Angeles, California, where he lives with his wife, Cherie, and their two daughters.

The next contribution I want to share with you is from William Paul Young, author of the book (which was also made into a movie) titled The Shack.

Communication Is an Exercise of Love
WILLIAM P. YOUNG

I have never heard God speak audibly. Some of my friends have, and I have no reason to doubt them. I assume

God is a good communicator, able to speak the entire cosmos into being with a single word. And I don't for a moment believe that God is distant and uncaring and does not take into consideration, out of love, our limitations; all that is broken in us which keeps us from hearing well. I believe this is why children have such an easier capacity for hearing God speak; they have less clutter and baggage and have usually not acquired or been forced to utilize survival skills to navigate life.

While I have never heard God speak audibly, I have heard the voice of God in a myriad of different ways. God has spoken in the voice of a friend, and sometimes an enemy; in the lyrics of a song, or in a rainstorm; in dreams, in imagination, in nudges and ideas; in a TV show or line in a movie; in the rise of unexpected emotions; inside tragedy and comfort, the voice of joy and wisdom as well as correction. As I said, God is a 'good' communicator, and that means both skilled and speaking from a good heart. Over the years of my life, conversation with God has moved from an external model to an internal one. I grew up with a God who was distant, and therefore communication was something projected 'out there' to heaven, or wherever I thought God was. I now am convinced this was one of the miscommunications of the religious environment in which I was raised.

We believed and taught separation, which I now consider to be an absolute myth. It took a long time to trust that God was 'in' me, that the communion of the Father, Son, and Holy Spirit was occurring 'in' me, that the Kingdom of God is 'within' me. Or as John 14:20 says, the three things the Holy Spirit is going to teach us are: "I (Jesus) am in the Father, and you are in me, and I am in you." Therefore, the primary place of communion and conversation is inside of us, because that is where God lives. Yes, all of creation is created in Jesus, so we live and move and have our being in Him, but that same

Jesus who holds the entire cosmos together dwells inside of you and me, along with the Father and the Spirit.

Inside is also where your false self (flesh) has been constructed by the lies you have believed, by the losses you have experienced, and by the messages you were told. So, the work of salvation is an internal work that then spills out onto the world and into the universe. We are designed to live from the inside out and not the outside in.

It is helpful to realize that often, God speaks to us in 'our' language, which we tend to discount because we believe we ought to hear God like someone else does, or our underlying shame whispers that only healthy, smart or righteous people can hear God speak. Often, I realize it was the voice of God in me in retrospect or hindsight. I can look back and recognize, after the fact, that in a specific moment it was God who was speaking to me. This is not an accusation, but evidence that we are learning and growing in our capacity to hear and recognize the voice of God in our lives. I believe God is speaking to us and listening to us all the time. In fact, the conversation between the Father, Son and Holy Spirit is happening in you. You are the temple of the Holy Spirit, the holy of holies. Give yourself some grace as you learn to distinguish the voice of God from your own, and from the voices of others. Learn to laugh at yourself, or with yourself. This is a process. Take the risk of sharing what you are hearing, but do so humbly, understanding that you might have been mistaken. I have a very dear friend who often says, when he is about to enter a deep conversation with someone, "I don't want anything that is precious to you at the beginning of this conversation to be less precious to you at the end." Communication is intended to be an exercising of love.

Let me tell you about one experience that altered my life considerably. Early in 2004, I realized that our family was headed toward a disastrous economic crisis, much of it because of the poor choices that I had made over many years that were coming to roost. It didn't help that our investments were tanking as well. It was a terrifying storm, and I could see it looming. Over the course of the preceding ten years, I had been working on learning how to trust, especially in God. When we are attempting to manage fear, our choice is either to trust or control, and my historic response to fear had been control. As a child, I had learned that trusting was dangerous, and my theology growing up had reinforced the idea that even God was fundamentally untrustworthy. Basically, I was on my own, especially when I was suffering the consequences of my own poor decisions. But over those ten years, my understanding of God had changed significantly, and I was learning slowly and incrementally how to choose trust rather than control.

But now in 2004, I was facing one of the deepest roots and darkest fears of my life, a fear that had driven me to control over and over: the fear of financial insecurity. Money represented a way to control without having to trust, and it took ten years to get that deep into my internal world. I decided to go on a fast, which is not a hunger strike to get God to feel bad enough for you to do something—the intention behind fasting is to hear with less distractions. For five days, I began a conversation each morning with, "Papa God, how come I have trusted you my whole life with our finances and we have been up and down, and up and down, and here we go again?" Five days in a row, I began my conversation with God by lying. On the fifth day, I began again. "Papa God, how come I have trusted you my whole life with our finances and we have been up and down, and up and down, and here we go again?" But this time I heard that still-small voice inside of me, not audible, but real, and basically, this is how the conversation went.

"Paul, are you ready to listen?"

"Why do you think I'm fasting?"

"Then listen! Paul, you have never trusted me 'your whole life' with anything, let alone your finances. Even when talking about that little piece of property and house you have been living on for the last seventeen years, you tell people I gave it to you, but I can't get my hands on it. Every time you begin to feel afraid and uncertain about your finances, you shade the truth, manipulate the relationship, and sometimes outright lie to save yourself."

Silence.

And then it hit me like a bolt of lightning, and I knew that what I was hearing was true. I began to weep, and weep, and weep. I confessed that what God was saying was true. I could think of many instances over the years when I had done exactly that. But now what was I supposed to do? Now that my self-deluding propensity to control was utterly exposed, what could I do to move into the risk of trust? By this time in my life, I had at least a dozen friends, men with whom I shared life. Their presence in my world was part of learning how to trust, and they had become a huge gift to me. I picked up the phone and called each of them, one at a time, and explained our situation. I knew that three of those twelve friends could have opened up a checkbook and, without hurting themselves whatsoever, written me a solution to our financial distress. After laying out what was happening in our financial world, I said to each of them, "I know you love my family, and I know you care for me, and you are guys, so I know you like to fix things. But please, please, please, don't rescue me from this. If you do, you will probably be interfering with something that God is trying to do in my life."

46

This was a response to what I had heard God say to me. The fast was over, and the trust was about to begin at a whole new level. That autumn, unbeknownst to me, seven of my guy friends took a day off from their work and came and sat with me at the County Courthouse while the County auctioned off the house in which my family and I had lived for seventeen years. The creditors took our cars and most of our material possessions. My friends helped us pack what we had left, and we moved to a little rental in the middle of five hundred acres of Christmas trees, and soon after that, into a tiny nine-hundred-square-foot rental in town so that I could walk to the train to get to one of my three jobs. God is far more concerned with healing our hearts than with our participation in some great plan to impact the world. In this instance, the loss of almost all our material possessions destroyed our fear of financial insecurity, and we learned how the opposite of 'more' is not 'less,' but 'enough.' We had been surrounded by 'enough' our whole life, but didn't know because we were living not in the present but rather creating future-tripping, fear-based imaginations of financial destruction and poverty.

We were living in the imagination of the future rather than in the presence of God. There is a God, who is Love, who lives in you, and therefore you are never alone. This God is a brilliant communicator and knows you, the unique and true you, and lives with you in the wonder of the everyday. Relax, grant yourself the grace you would to anyone else whom you love, and give yourself to the One who is good and trustworthy and speaks to you in an infinite number of ways.

To find out more about Paul Young, check out http://www.wmpaulyoung.com.

William Paul Young was born in Canada and raised among a Stone Age tribe by his missionary parents in the highlands of former New Guinea. He suffered great loss as a child and young adult and now enjoys the "wastefulness of grace" with his family in the Pacific Northwest. He is the author of *Lies We Believe About God* and the *New York Times* bestsellers *The Shack, Cross Roads,* and *Eve.*

Often, people think it is challenging or impossible to include God in business, but I beg to differ, and Bob Hasson is one of those people who helps us see how we can bridge that gap. Bob not only owns and runs one of the largest painting companies in the United States, he also hears from God as he works. Listen to what he has to say.

Hearing God in Business
BOB HASSON

I have spent my career in a highly demanding business, and I have met a lot of people who think God does not want to speak into business, or that what God says is not relevant to business. Nothing could be further from the truth! I am seeing God speak and move in business every day. I have been blessed to see God partner with businessmen and women and inspire them to walk in their calling and be the hands and feet of God by providing a reasonable service.

When I think of how God speaks in business, I think first to how we (as people made in God's image) speak to each other. We as people do not only speak audibly. We speak with our body language, we sense what others are thinking and feeling, we speak through text and written words, we speak through others sometimes as well. No matter the mode, good communication exists on a foundation of closeness, trust and intimacy. The more we spend time with a person, the more their way of thinking and speaking impacts us. I do not think it is any different with God. God speaks in myriad ways, and we get the joy of engaging with Him on every level and seeing His words manifest in our lives as we pursue closeness, trust and intimacy with Him. I am excited to share with you just four of the ways God speaks to me while I am doing business. I hope they will inspire you to hear God in your career as well.

The first way I hear from God is by having a lifestyle of letting God transform me. I am transformed by the relationship with Him so that I can sense, know, and execute His words and heart in any given situation. One example of this is that I used to think the voice of God was the same as the critical voice of my own earthly father. These words in my own thoughts made it harder to do business, to have the courage to take chances. I was terrified of failing, and the critical words would flood my own head if I thought I'd failed. But as I spent time with God and in fellowship with Him, asking Him about this, I realized He was not the angry or critical voice in my head. He wanted to transform my thoughts with words of unconditional love and acceptance in every situation. This changed me dramatically, because I had constant access to His words of love, grace, and pride in me as His son. No longer did I have the pressure to perform well in order to feel good enough. My relationships became stronger because I was more secure, and I made much better business decisions because I was not operating out of fear of punishment. I was able to stop hiding and show up fully and powerfully as the person God made me to be in a business deal, in how I responded to my team and employees, even in how I fired people!

A second way I hear from God is through His written word. In my study times, I internalize His word. I digest it so it can nourish my soul to help me live a life where I have strength and direction for every situation. I try to surround myself with the Word until I become one with the Word instead of simply expressing the Word. I must study to understand what is in God's heart, so that I can have access to it in the moments that are hard, or the moments when I need help, or when I have to make decisions. An example of how God often uses this to speak to me is that I will get reminders of His words and scriptures when I need direction, or need help to know which choice to make. God gives us Biblical messages in his Word, and the Holy Spirit brings it to life in real time to me so I know I can apply his words to certain situations and get the best outcome.

Thirdly, God speaks through others. Sometimes, God's Word comes through another human. In this situation, we need discernment to hear God. Sometimes what others say is wisdom and makes sense, but it is the wrong wisdom for a situation. Other times it might be directly from God, even if it does not make complete sense. Being humble and being willing to hear what God speaks to me thought my wife, kids and team members is crucial, because we are all the body of Christ and we need each other to hear the whole story. I remember one time when I was frustrated with a legal situation and one of my team members told me I needed to stop fighting and settle the deal. I weighed this in my heart, and I believe it was God's Word for me in the moment. I challenge you to keep your ears open to the people in your life. They may be carrying messages from God!

Finally, sometimes I know God is speaking because I get a very strong sense leading me to do something I would never do—something that defies logic or reason or what my own experience would say to do. In one situation, I went into a negotiation and something just felt different. I usually lead the negotiations, but this time I felt I had to be quiet. After being quiet for some time, the leader on the other end got up and asked me to go into a private meeting room with him. He started making offers, and I felt very strongly that I should not respond, but instead just doodle on a notepad. This is not something I would normally do! It defies all logic and the human negotiation wisdom I have learned over the years. But I followed this promoting, and the negotiator continued to raise what my team would be paid, until finally I was offered the price I wanted. I could have used my negotiating skills, and maybe I would have gotten a good contract, but maybe not. Either way, it increased my faith that God can and does enter situations with us, and like with shadrach, meshach and abednego, God is standing with us in the fires of business and negotiation, even if others cannot see Him. I knew that it was from the LORD because it was not something I have ever done nor would recommend to do, but I felt at peace about it. I felt grace for it. Recognizing the grace of God and tapping into that is something that will lead to partnering with God for transformation.

I see God's word come alive in my day and impact everything about me, my relationships, and how I run my business. We cannot limit God to one way of speaking. Imagine if you only spoke to your spouse with words, or only with body language, or text. The relationship would not be nearly as dynamic or meaningful, would it? It wouldn't be able to impact you or transform you as much. It is the same with God. His Word is there to create transformation and Heaven on earth as I negotiate contracts, hire a new employee, or give a raise to an employee who has been with me for twenty years.

To find out more about Bob Hasson, check out http://www.bobhasson.com

Bob Hasson is a businessman and leadership consultant. His greatest passion is strengthening leaders and their organizations, with specific focus on developing sound organizational structure, fiscal responsibility, and dynamic relationships on leadership teams. As CEO of R.M Hasson Painting Contractors, Inc., which he founded in 1978, he established the company as a trusted partner, serving general contractors across the Western United States. Since 2012, he has traveled around the world with Danny Silk as a speaker and consultant for Loving on Purpose. He has been married for thirty years to his wife, Lauren, and is the proud father of David, Kyler, Isabella and Sophia.

Jeremy Butrous has spent his career working for, and with, prophetic ministries world-wide. He creates content, products, resources, marketing strategies, and events that help others encounter God. Here is what he has to say about hearing God's voice and how it impacts his daily life.

Hearing God Through Your Options
JEREMY BUTROUS

Daily, we live in a perplexing mystery of humanity. We find ourselves trying to understand situations, relationships and life with a limited perspective and personal shortcomings. Yet, we have been given options. We don't just have the "good option" or the "better option"; we also have the option of "best." Best is presented and vocalized through God's Word, present in the established (logos) Word of God and reinforced and communicated through the (rhema) Word of God spoken by Him into my life on a daily basis.

When a situation presents itself, I am never without options. The option to select the most perfected and best possible outcome. If I miss it in any way, I am provided with the most perfected redemptive option because of God's voice established though his nature and the will of God walked out through Jesus. His present voice is delivered through the invitation of my request; He never forces his voice on me. He is never demanding or controlling, but He is supportive and servant-hearted toward the success of my life. God speaks daily by presenting options and helping me be aware of them.

To find the best options for my life, I must walk out a relational journey of connecting with God, because He has a multitude of options for every one of my situations. He sees me where I am at in my life, and he goes outside of time, looks deep past my current situation into the realm of possibility somewhere in the future that exists in him. He brings the option back to me and presents it to me in the moment I am living. He does this in a way that is relational, so that I have to pursue him and realize that in him is my answer, in him is my best future and my hope. I realize my answer in the midst of the mystery of humanity that I live in.

Choosing God's option in my daily life is choosing transformation and empowerment for my life. A suitable example comes to mind. A while back I experienced a deep relational betrayal. I do not know if you have experienced deep betrayal before, but it shakes you to the core of who you are. When you have built your life around certain relationships, the betrayal is on many layers, and too deep for words to express. I was presented the option to collect the negative thoughts, the negative emotional experiences, to build a case against God, or people, to become bitter, to become closed off in my heart and my mind.

Instead, I began to go to my relationship with God for help, dialoguing with Him in an open discussion. I chose not to engage in broken prayer, which is a one-way street. I knew

He cared more about my wellbeing than I did myself. In the midst of my prayerful enquiry, I was asking God what He thought, and the way He felt about my situation. I asked Him what He thought about that person, and what He thought about me. He presented me with His perspective. It was not an audible voice, but it was so powerful and so outside of my own thoughts that I felt I was hearing His thoughts as clearly as if someone were standing in front of me and speaking to me. God shared the moment of betrayal where He had been betrayed by that person before they betrayed me. He shared the time and the moment it happened, shared the betrayal He experienced all the way back on the cross. How He felt, and what He was thinking, how He chose to love this person despite it, and how He chose His option of how to respond. In that very moment, the deep pain and emotional baggage I was feeling was put into check with the most relatable person that ever existed: JESUS! I choose, through prayer, to think positively and compassionately about the person, pray for them, and release for them the forgiveness that God has requested me to provide. Choosing the redemptive option God spoke to me played out for me as it did for Job in the Bible. Everything I lost was multiplied, or improved, and then given back to me. In a strange way, the betrayal was a gateway to be more blessed than I ever was before, only because of God's word. Hearing and being aware of the options Jesus provided me in my pain allowed me to be released into the abundance and reward of Jesus in a life-transforming way. I will never find someone who is more relatable or more helpful than Jesus. I find him at home, at work and in the world around me.

Invite Him in and provide Him with the vulnerability to affect you. Just give Him the opportunity to love you, to care for you, in every decision and in every way. Everything will be so different. The option to follow His way and model may transform you, or it may redeem you. It doesn't matter our context or situation. In all areas of life, in the greatest successes that we could potentially achieve, and in the lowest places that we find ourselves, God answers the mystery of our humanity with His action-filled, intentional voice that brings us the perfect, most redemptive option. Sometimes, we miss it. Sometimes we thought we knew, but we heard wrong, or we felt like going a certain way, but we incorrectly discerned, or we were deceived or misled by someone else.

Regardless of how we got to a place of lack or perceived failure, God instills, within every moment that exists in time, a timeless, redemptive option. It is only through the nature of God that we find ourselves saved. If we believe in Him, He will provide a timeless, everlasting, relational connection to His nature. Inside that connection is the redemptive work of Christ. That is not set aside for tomorrow, in Heaven, or a distant eternity, but it is ever-present and available yesterday, today and forever. His nature is spoken about in John when Jesus declares that the Kingdom of Heaven is at hand. The Word of God is made flesh and has dwelt among us; God desires for the embodiment of His nature to be ever-present in our day, providing us with the will, the heart, the mind of God. The most beautiful thing about the cross is that it provides us with redemptive options for our past. Even though a standard may be set, our situation may be true, our bad prognosis may be factually correct—God provides us with a redemptive option.

God not only wants to go deep into the heart of our future and present us with something that brings us closer to our calling in the moment, but He also wants to go deep into our past and rewrite the areas of missed opportunity, pain, and real or perceived failure so that it becomes part of what leads us to our new best option. His ever-present voice provides us with a redemptive and best-case scenario all in one. That is because he lives in yesterday, he lives in today, and he lives in forever, right now. We serve a God outside of time. So let us connect with the nature of God through Revelation 19:10 so that we may see the testimony of Jesus in our lives every day!

Jeremy Butrous
www.jeremybutrous.com

Jeremy's life passion is seeing people transformed and changed through the power of God. After completing the three-year Bethel School of Supernatural Ministry in Redding, California, he focused his career on empowering speakers and authors to create resources and events that support the body of Christ world-wide. He and his wife, Ally, run a consulting business for authors and speakers called Radiant Thoughts. They also co-host a podcast by the same name, which explores relational, emotional, spiritual and financial prosperity from a Biblical perspective. He is the author of several books, including *Transcending Mindsets* and *Praying Through The Seven Mountains*. Jeremy and Ally enjoy living in Los Angeles with their bichon-poodle, Pepper.

God's Voice Lines Up With God's Nature
KASEY FULLER:

Learning to hear God's voice can be quite an interesting journey. I learned this early on as a baby Christian. First, let me start off by saying that I got saved at the young age of nineteen, and had been going to church my entire life. With that said, there had been many times in my life when I felt the presence of God, and even encountered Him, and I just knew that it was Him. For example, when I was around the age of twelve, I was in a very desperate situation where I was being sexually abused by my step-father (for three years at that point in time), and I was ready to die. I was planning my suicide, and I knew I couldn't continue to live like this any longer. It was at that time that I heard God in my spirit say, "Kasey, I am with you, and I will never leave you. You have a purpose. Trust me." I felt a peace come over me like I had never felt before, and I knew I had to go on. The voice of the Holy Spirit quite literally saved my life. As I said before, I went to church, but at that time, I truly had not committed my life to the Lord yet. I talked to Him sometimes, and I wanted to know Him, but for me it was a long journey from there to my salvation day.

About ten years later, after I had received the Lord as my savior, and I was walking with Him, and going deeper in my personal relationship with Him. I began to experience more of Him, and what I call a "training period" where I began to hear His voice more clearly. I was a young mother and wife at this time, and had definitely had a few other instances where I heard the Lord, and I knew it was His voice, but I certainly was not in tune to that on a day-to-day basis by any means. For example, when Jon and I first got married, we were nineteen and twenty at the time, and when I began serving the Lord I had a pretty intense encounter that forever changed the way I viewed God. I was told I may never be able to conceive, and had a miscarriage very early on.

I began to pray and I remember telling the Lord, "Please heal me from this. What happened to me was not my sin, and you are my Father." I remember telling Jon I am asking the Lord to completely heal me. At that time, we had a traveling evangelist who had been speaking at our church for several weeks, and we were attending regularly. One evening, Jon and I went up to the altar and we were just sitting on the steps praying together. All of a sudden I felt a crippling pain in my stomach, and I bent over. Then, the evangelist got up and went the microphone and said, "God is healing somebody's womb right now." I instantly looked up at Jon, and said "God just healed me." I knew it was Him. My Abba Father showing me how good He truly is, and that He is always with me just like He said. Afterward, Jon went up to the evangelist and he said, "Kasey received that healing tonight," and he replied, "Well, congratulations, Daddy." I was pregnant with my oldest daughter about two weeks after this encounter. This really catapulted me into my journey of hearing God's voice.

I wanted to know, and I had so many questions. How do I know if it's you I'm really hearing? What's the difference between you saying something to me, and my own conscious? Thus began my training period. I heard the Lord say, "I am going to teach you to hear my voice, and you will know that it's me." I wasn't so sure about this, because it sounded like my own voice. First, I had to recognize that the basis for knowing God's voice and being assured that it is Him has to begin in a place of understanding who He is, and never straying from the truth of scripture.

The bible says in Hebrews 13:8 that God is the same yesterday, today and forever, so we know if something is contrary to this it is not of Him. Secondly, we have to recognize that we were created to commune with God. His original intent in Genesis was to walk with us daily, to have relationship, and that has never changed. His Holy Spirit is inviting us to go deeper into this relationship with Him, and He will take us as deep as we want to go. As I began to understand who God was, that He was good, He loved me, He had good plans for me, and He was loving, kind, patient, long suffering, graceful and peaceful, it began to transform me. I realized that the voices I heard that did not line up with God's nature were not God at all. So what were they? Some of them were my own thoughts, my own ideas, my own pain. Then I began to recognize that we have an enemy. Ephesians 6:16 says, "In addition to all this, take up the shield of faith with which you can extinguish all the fiery darts of the evil one." 1 Peter 5:8 says "Be alert and of sober mind. Your enemy the devil prowls around like a roaring lion looking for someone to devour." What does that mean? That means that not everything I think is my thought. That means that I am at war with an enemy who will not always be there for me, does not love me, and is the opposite in nature of Jesus Christ. So any thought I have that does not line up with His nature may even be an attack of the enemy, and most likely is! That being said, I want to stay on track to hearing God's voice, and what that looks like. I began to realize very quickly that a lot of the time when I hear the Lord speak, it goes against my actual nature, possibly even what I feel like I want to do, and always lines up with His word and who He is. A time that stands out to me was during this training time when I left the house in the evening to go to the grocery store. Jon was home and we had two children at the time, and it was starting to get dark outside. At this time, we owned a health food store, and it was directly across the street from the grocery store. As I was coming out of the grocery store I thought to myself that I needed to run in there and get something I had left earlier in the day. I don't even remember what it was now, maybe a jacket or something simple like that, but I heard the Holy Spirit say, "Don't go in there right now." Mind you, it was closed, and I was just trying to get stuff done, because I'm a doer. I automatically thought to myself "This is ridiculous. This is not the Lord. This is totally me. Just go in there and get it, and it's done."

Again, I heard the Holy Spirit say, "Don't go in there right now." So what did I do? I ignored it, and went in there anyway of course. Once I got in, I put in the code to unlock the alarm, locked the door behind me, and grabbed my item. As I turned around to leave I could see over in the shadows behind the grocery store that a very scary-looking man was staring in the window, watching my every move. I began to feel quite a bit of fear come over me, and I knew I just needed to get out quick, get to my car, and get home. As I approached the door to unlock it with the key (this was years ago so it was a very difficult lock) it would not turn to unlock. So not only was this guy staring at me, and making me feel very uncomfortable, I could not open the door to get out. I stood there turning it, fighting with it for several minutes. Then, I walked over to the phone and called Jon. He was telling me all the tricks to try, and none were working. I finally hung up with him and almost began to cry. I heard the Holy Spirit speak to me. "This is why I didn't want you to come in here tonight. To protect you from all of this." I realized that I had clearly heard His voice, and right away I repented. I said, "Lord, forgive me for not paying attention to you." I went over to the door, and it immediately opened. I ran to my car and left. I learned a very valuable lesson that day about trusting the Lord completely. Proverbs 3:5-6 is one of my favorite verses to this day. "Trust in The Lord with all your heart, and lean not on your own understanding. In all your ways acknowledge Him, and He will direct your paths." He wants to invade every part of our lives, and He wants us to trust Him completely. No matter where you are on this journey of hearing God's voice, I want to encourage you to go deeper, and know that He is saying to you, "I am always with you, I will never leave you."

To find out more about Kasey Fuller, check out fullerlifeandfitness.com or rureal.org.

Kasey has a passion for health, fitness, and the overall picture of what a healthy lifestyle looks like. As a Certified Personal Trainer, she is passionate about helping others reach their goals and walk out a life that is all-around healthy: spirit, soul and body. Kasey's biggest accomplishment is being a mother to three beautiful children, and being a wife to her amazing husband. They have worked together to create and live a healthy, balanced lifestyle God's way.

Wow! I don't know about you, but when I read at all these ways God speaks, I am amazed and start to feel that the possibilities to hear God are endless! From just doing daily life with God, to getting impressions, or understanding how God relates to our situations, we can hear and experience God in so many deeply personal ways that may have nothing to do with an audible voice.

I encourage you to stop here and reflect on your own journey of hearing God before we continue. How do you experience God, and what in these stories surprised you? Take some time in prayer to see what God is speaking and quickening in your heart even now, and allow it to marinate and sink in so that your connection with God grows stronger and you can truly begin to partner with Him to transform your life.

Transforming Steps:

1. Which of the stories above stood out to you the most? What do you think God is trying to tell you though that story?
2. What is one new way you learned that you can hear from God?
3. Were there any ways you now realize you have heard from God, but maybe did not know it was Him at the time?

Chapter Four

CREATING YOUR TRUE IDENTITY WITH GOD

"Do you know who you are? I think one of the deepest questions of our existence is to find out who we are and what we are supposed to do. Maybe we start to realize we have purpose and exist for a reason, but we look in the wrong places and to the wrong people for answers. Here is a story to illustrate. Recently, we bought a cash register from a previous owner for our coffee shop and it didn't come with instructions. There were a lot of functions and keys I had no idea what to do with. I started to become frustrated, and at that point looked up the make and model on Google to see what I could come up with. I think life is a lot like this process. Like my cash register, we look to others for answers to fix the problems we have.

What we really need is the original manufacturer to tell us how we were built and designed. The reason so many people struggle with who they are is because they've allowed other people to tell them who they are and what their life should look like. Their spirit inside of them knows something isn't right and they have the wrong brand on them, and it creates an internal frustration. Their spirit in them and their soul are telling them two different things, causing an internal struggle that only God can solidify.

But, thankfully, God put the longing for identity in us because it is important for us to know who we are. He knows exactly who we are, and in order for us to learn and operate out of who we are made to be, we need His help! Only He knows how we are built, inside and out. He knows everything about us.

Discovering Your True Identity

Our identity is made up of different things. We are so unique that phone makers are able to use our fingerprints and eye scans to open our phones up. These are very specific things that define us, that are on the outside of course. Our identity goes deeper though, it is made up of our core beliefs, our thoughts about ourselves, our values, and so much more. But even that is still almost surface if you don't realize where you came from and where you are going.

On this journey, it's more than just stepping into our purpose, gifts, talents and destiny. It's about discovering who God is. It's about relationship and cultivating intimacy with Him. This was always the original plan. When we go back to Genesis, we see that was how God intended it to be. Genesis 1:27 says, "So God created man in his own image, in the image of God he created him; male and female he created them." (ESV) We are made in His image, so to fully understand our identity, we must address that we are designed to be like Him. Not just to be like him, but to imitate Him. (Ephesians 5:1)

Genesis 3:8 says that God walked with Adam in the cool of the day. They had cultivated time together, and Adam got to know God. The reason this is so important is because if we were made in the image of God, we will operate best when we take on the characteristics of Christ and have the fruits of the Holy Spirit in our lives. But, we can't have any of these things if we don't know where we came from, or the God whose image we were made in! But how we do this is another question. Jesus is our example, because sin has never come into His life and thwarted His design or image.

In my first book, *Remodel Your Life,* I talk about how Jesus is the ultimate remodeler. We are these broken-down old houses that may have built our identity on the sandy foundation of a challenging childhood, or negative life experiences. Or maybe there was a good foundation, but we have allowed time and weather to destroy and take away from our original design and beauty.

When it comes to building a home, the most important thing you start with is a foundation. Everything after this process goes on top of it. If it is not built right, or solid, it will cause everything else to crack and/or fall apart. The same goes with us. We can have all the talent and gifts the world has ever seen, but if our foundation isn't built on the characteristics of Christ and who He is, then eventually everything will fall apart.

This is why spending time with Jesus and allowing the Holy Spirit into our lives is the most essential thing we could do if we are trying to understand who we are. I like to think of identity as being like a burrito—you take all of who you are, like your gifts, talents, life experiences and personality, and you wrap it all up in Jesus. He is the very thing that holds us all together and makes us what we are. If you and I are made in the image of God and we are supposed to represent Him and be like Him, then we need to see a role model. We have never been able to see God's perfect design because we came into a sinful world. What we need is a perfect example so we know how to step into what we were created to be. That perfect example is Jesus. Christ is the only person who can make us into a new creation full of purpose and identity. In 2 Corinthians 5:17 ESV, we read, "Therefore, if anyone is in

Christ, he is a new creation. The old has passed away; behold, the new has come."

Not only has He shown us a way, but He allows us to enter into that way! Galatians 2:20 says, "I have been crucified with Christ. It is no longer I who live, but Christ who lives in me. And the life I now live in the flesh I live by faith in the Son of God, who loved me and gave himself for me." (ESV)

Jesus said in John 5:19 that He only did what He saw His Father doing and only spoke what the Father was saying. When I see Jesus, I see a man like me, but one who has no lack. Jesus had everything He needed when He was on this earth. I know it wasn't a coincidence that when Jesus started His ministry and got baptized, the Father spoke and said, "This is my son in whom I am well pleased."

The Father rolls up on the scene to love on His son. Jesus knew where He came from and who His Father was. Because of this, He walked in the authority of who His Father created Him to be. When you know who you are, where you're going, and who your Father is, it makes it easy to walk in authority from on high.

Jesus says in John 10:10, "I came that they may have life and have it abundantly." These words and actions are a picture of who He is and how He thinks of us. Since our birth, we have lived in sin. The world around us has fallen and been subjected to things God never intended for us or creation. It has always been God's plan to restore us back into His original design, to be a people that walked with Him through life and are dearly loved.

Learning God's Identity

God never needed us, but He chose us. God is confident in who He is and states that very clearly throughout the

Word when He gives us His names. We also should walk in confidence knowing where we come from, who our Father is, and that we are ambassadors of our Father's kingdom.

I want to dig into this for a moment, because God did not just give Himself all these names because he was confused or bored. God used His names to describe His nature, and by knowing His nature, we learn more about ourselves. When Moses met God on the mountain, God told him, " I AM who I AM." There is no lack in God; therefore, he doesn't need anything because He is the source of all things. As we read about the different names of God, I think it clearly shows us not just who God is, but how He sees himself.

There were several names that God gave us to give us a picture or a partial picture of who He is.

For example, God is called Jehovah. This name shows us that God is complete, not lacking anything, nor does He change. He is a God who keeps His word, today, yesterday, or forever. As we imitate Him, we are invited into His completeness! We do not lack a sense of identity. No other God has this name. God is all things good.

Another name for God is Jehovah-jireh. God calls Himself to be a provider through this name. This name was used when God provided an alternative sacrifice to Abraham, so he did not have to sacrifice his son Isaac. God provided a ram out of nowhere on the mountain to be a sacrifice, the same way he provided Jesus to cover our sins and enable us to reconnect to God. God can provide us all things because He created all and He is all. There is no lack in Him and He is infinite.

God is also called Jehovah-shalom. This name means "the God of peace." If you have ever spent any time in the presence of God, you've experienced this. There's nothing like it and it takes away every worry, doubt and fear that has come against your mind. To be like God is to be in peace. Isaiah 26:3 says, "You keep him in perfect peace, whose mind is stayed on you, because he trusts in you." (ESV) To have an identity in God is to have a right to peace in both our minds and hearts.

God is also Jehovah-rophe. This name means "Jehovah heals." When I think of this, I can't help but be overwhelmed by gratitude and thankfulness. I have seen God heal my wife to have kids, restore my mind, and heal our hearts. God takes what the world has tried to destroy and builds beauty out of ashes. NO ONE can do what He is able to do in our hearts and minds. So, to be like God is to be healed and able to help be His hands and feet to bring healing to others. This may be through prayer, medicine, or encouragement to a broken heart, but regardless of the avenue, healing is part of our identity.

As we go through the Bible, there are so many names that give us a picture of who He is and His identity. We can look around at all mankind and catch glimpses of who He is in others. I encourage you, if you feel you are lacking identity, to study the names of God. You will find a lot of good information there to help realign you. Because we all need realignment. Identity is a funny thing—how we see ourselves and who we really are don't always align, unfortunately. We often see this with the Israelites in the Bible.

Getting Rid of Your Old Identity

I recently was reading the book of Numbers in the Old Testament and was taken back by the Israelites' reaction to what God had done for them. If you're not familiar with the story, I will give you a brief recap (Jon Fuller's version of it, anyway). You can find the real thing in the Bible. So, the story I am thinking of starts when the Israelites had been slaves among the Egyptians for four hundred years. They cried out to God to be delivered, and God sent them Moses to lead them to the promise land He had for them.

During the process of their exodus, they had seen the most amazing historical events in history happen before their eyes. God fought the most powerful army in the world on their behalf to set them free. God sent plagues and natural disasters to destroy the Egyptians. They literally had to do nothing but obey what He told them to do. If that wasn't enough and impossible for any human to accomplish, during their walk to the promised land, the Egyptian army had the Israelites pinned between them and the Red sea. God again pulled off a "Only God could do this" and split the sea in half. They walked through it and the sea devoured the army. Talk about God being our defender, wow! So I just recapped the whole "Prince of Egypt" movie for you if you didn't have any reference. I don't remember if the movie is totally accurate, so read your Bible, then watch the movie.

Back to my point on identity, God just blew up the whole scene on their behalf, delivered them from the impossible, and now we get to the point where I want to throat punch myself. Yes, I mean that. Moses sent out spies to go look at the land that God promised them. Did I say promise? He had fulfilled everything so far and done wonders they had never seen. The spies came back and besides Joshua and Caleb, they all told them they couldn't take the land. The land was everything God promised and better than they had imagined, but there were giants in the land. The spies thought the giants would crush them like bugs or something to that effect. When I read the story, I'm just blown away. This is a very powerful story that you need to read from start to finish, but there's one thing you need to take away from this.

68

The Egyptians had beaten them for hundreds of years, starved them, and even killed them. The Israelites had mentally been beaten down for generations, so that even in the midst of God doing wonders, they forgot who they were. Their identity had become what Egypt had beaten into them. Even in their deliverance and process of healing, they wouldn't trust God. Because of this rebellion and distrust toward God, they brought Him to anger and they never saw their promise. Now their children did, and the promise was fulfilled, but because they disobeyed (aka, they chose what God told them was not in their best interest) they missed out on something they could have experienced with their kids. God had chosen them just like He chose you and me. If you look around you, there are miracles and things you can't explain that have happened your whole life. God wants us to come into a place of understanding that we ARE HIS Children, not the world's. He has set us apart and has love and goodness toward us that we will never be able to comprehend. It is our job and responsibility to receive that and walk in it.

A lady recently spoke to my wife and I and said the following, which rang so true: Don't take your peasant to the castle, take your princess to the streets. It is so easy to allow our past to dictate and tell us who we are, but the truth is that's not who we are. We are no longer the children of the past, God says in 2 Corinthians 5:17, "For if a man belongs to Christ, he is a new person. The old life is gone. New life has begun." I'm a new man in Christ, that the old is gone and the new has come. I challenge you to walk in the new. The old will only bring you death, since you died with Christ, and the new is raised to life. That scripture tells me that the old me can only bring forth dead things, and like the Israelites, if you chose to walk in that you will miss your promise.

So, we find our identity in who God is, and what he has done, but we also can find our identity in who He says we

69

are, and what He says about us. If He is the truth, and He is eternal, and He is peace and provider, what He says about us and our life matters. I have personally gone through the Bible and written down the things that God says I am, and I would encourage you to do the same.

One night recently I felt moved to write down thirty days of affirmations from the scripture. These were things that I could speak over myself that God says I am. It doesn't have to be complicated—simply coming up with affirmations you can speak over yourself to help create that reality in your spirit and soul. Things such as, "I am found, I am loved, I am saved, I am Gentle, I am anointed, I have purpose, I am delivered, I am blessed." This washing of our mind in the Word helps to transform us to have victory in our understanding of our identity. Using whole scriptures can also be helpful. I like 1 Peter 2:9, which says, "But you are a chosen race, a royal priesthood, a holy nation, a people for his own possession, that you may proclaim the excellencies of him who called you out of darkness into his marvelous light." (ESV) Talk about a verse loaded with identity!

Why speak these things, though? Why not just think them? Well, remember that words hold transformative power in them. Remember Luke 6:25, which states that whatever is in your heart comes out in your words, and we are also affected by what we hear and choose to believe and speak over ourselves. As we speak God's promises over us and allow them to go into our hearts and minds, we start to realize that's who we are and were always supposed to be. It's a beautiful process of transformation, like a caterpillar turning into a butterfly. God wraps us up in His word and transforms us into who He designed us to be, something beautiful.

70

It Doesn't Stop With You

But I want to make another point here, which is that we are not just called to find our own identity, but to help others in the world to find theirs! God gives us our identity, as people made in His image, and He gives us the power to create identity in others through the power of words and actions. This is why words hurt. They can cut to and shake our very identity. How many of us are still hanging onto negative or hurtful things people said to us when we were kids, things we still feel we have to run from? And this is why we are called to speak words of life and not death over each other. Because those words matter!

As I'm sitting here in my cold closet writing this, I can't help but to think of words as gas to a fire. Maybe because I'm cold. Negative words spoken in my life or to someone else are like gas thrown on a wild forest fire. They're not intended for that purpose and are causing the problem to get worse for those around them—they are destructive. They burn a trail behind them and cause scarring that can take years to heal. But a fire in the right place can bring warmth and comfort.

A couple years ago, I built a rock fireplace in my backyard so that we could all hang out and roast marshmallows. My son and I got some wood and started to pile it up in there, and we didn't have much time for it to get started so I went and got the gas can. For whatever reason, my mind was occupied as I was pouring the gas on, and I just kept on adding. A gallon might be an over-exaggeration but regardless of how much I added, it was too much for what we needed. I bent over to light the match right next to the pit (not sure why I did that either) and BOOM! We had a fire. It blew me back a couple feet and the flame was about eight to ten feet high. We had a bonfire in our backyard, where I meant to have something small. I looked over to my son to remind him that's what you don't do in a residential area. For all of you out there thinking how irresponsible I was, I want to assure you I did have a fire extinguisher and a water hose running right next to us as we did this. After all that, we had a blast (literally) and got to hang out for hours enjoying each other's conversation, eating s'mores, and getting warmth. Our words can have that effect on our life and on others around us. They can be the catalyst to a life of abundance. Sometimes, all we need is God's word (gas) and a little spark, and off we go.

Who Do You Let Speak Into Your Identity?

It is important whom we let speak into our identity and that we guard it. God taught me a truth about identity through a Disney movie, of all things. The story of Cinderella is the story of a loved child, who had all kinds of terrible and negative things spoken about her and to her. Her identity as a loved daughter was crushed, but she did not give up hope. I will never forget several years ago when the movie *Cinderella* came out and I took my family to go see it. There was the part when Cinderella pulls up to the castle in the most amazing glowing blue carriage with strong-looking horses that represent royalty and strength. This is her true identity, and she is finally walking in it because (somewhat ironically) of the words her Fairy Godmother speaks over her.

The castle is all decked out in all its splendor for the royal ball, and the door opens for her to get out. As the door opens, the perspective moves to inside the carriage, as if you too were in the carriage, about to step out, and I hear Holy Spirit say, "Are you ready to step into your destiny"? Oh my gosh, it took everything I had not to fall apart in the movie theater! It was as if He was reminding me to shed the old identity and step into the truth of my identity in Him! Not only did I just hear that, but I could feel the presence of God all over me. Now truth be told, I'm a total crier when it comes to movies—I hate to say it, but it's true. My family knows it, and sometimes it gives all of us a good laugh. I was doing everything I could to keep it together, and it was not because of Cinderella. As tears started rolling down my face at this Disney princess movie, my wife looked over at me and asked me if I was okay. It wasn't like something significant had happened in the movie to warrant such tears.

What she didn't know was God had just shown up and completely rocked me. He spoke my identity over me through the story and images. It was a demonstration of His word to my spirit and a reminder that no words spoken against me could stand in the way of my destiny, unless I let them. Cinderella could have given into the lies and become angry and bitter, and never received her destiny. How many Cinderellas are living around you now? How many need some words from you to empower them and speak into them and their calling?

I've been told that money tellers can detect fake money because they handle real currency all the time. They are trained to look for certain things, but handling the real thing day in and day out helps them to easily detect something fake. The negative words we think and speak are much like fake money. I like to think of God's Word as Heaven's currency. As we handle His word daily and speak it out loud, it "buys" what we get in life. Please don't misunderstand what I'm saying—I don't mean like some hocus-pocus, Harry-Potter-type experience. I don't just start saying words, command a million dollars to appear, and poof, I have it. That is not what I mean. To get Heaven's currency, we have to go to the bank of Heaven and go to the teller. Only the Father and creator of our life has the words for us to speak.

So, I will go back to my question at the start of the chapter: Do you know who you are? No matter where you are at in your personal identity journey, all you need to know to start your journey is that our identity comes from the maker. No one knows us better than He who made us. All of us have a foundation we can start from, and those are found in God's word. The rest of the process is like a treasure hunt of self-discovery and finding the treasures He buried inside of us, and then declaring that truth in our mind and life.

When I was a kid, I loved Legos. I still remember building castles, spaceships and everything else in between. I enjoyed them because you could take these little pieces, and as you kept on adding them together you would eventually end up with something really cool. When you were finished, you would have a sense of accomplishment and you could enjoy your hard work.

God's Word is the instruction book telling us who we are. His word is both the things he speaks through the Bible and the things He tells me directly through the time I spend with Him. These are like the Legos He gives me to build something one step at a time, according to His plan. All I have to do is take His Word (or words) and start speaking them over myself to build the life He created me to have.

I know from experience, as we start our transformation journey, things will come up that could stall us, or get in our way. In the first chapters, I shared about the tools we have to transform our lives: words, love, hearing God and discovering our identity. In the next three chapters, I want to shift the conversation, and discuss how to overcome some of the biggest roadblocks that we will come across as we pursue these things. These roadblocks are disobedience, fear, and disconnecting the natural and supernatural. I am excited to have you on this journey and hope the next few chapters will empower you to overcome the fiery darts of the enemy, to overcome His schemes and achieve the transformation God has for you!

Transforming Steps:

1. Re-read some of the names of God that are discussed in this chapter. What do you need more of in your life?
2. Who does God say that you are? Take some time to really ask Him who He says you are—not what your thoughts or experiences say, but what HE says. Write these down and dwell on them. Is someone speaking into your identity who does not agree with God's words spoken over you? Take steps to dismiss their voice.
3. What are some affirmations from the Scripture that you can speak over yourself daily to help shape your new identity?

Chapter Five

OBEDIENCE: OUR TRANSFORMATION POWER

"The word obedience for most people has a negative connotation. They might even call it a "trigger word" that creates a cascade of negative or uncomfortable feelings. Most people definitely would not think of the word "obedience" as a synonym for "transformation." If they did, the transformation is only out of a place of fear. But God is Love, and 1 John 4:18 in the New International Version says, "There is no fear in love. But perfect love drives out fear, because fear has to do with punishment. The one who fears is not made perfect in love." Obedience is not about control or fear at all; it is about trust and an upgraded life.

What Is Obedience, REALLY?

When I think of obedience, I think of it as a key that will get you where you want to go and get you to the person you were created to be. But it wasn't always like that. In the past, obedience was very hard for me, for two reasons. First, I had been wounded so deeply by people close to me that I had a hard time trusting that God not just loved me, but cared for me. I projected an idea that he was trying to boss me around or control me to do something not in my best interest, because I had seen people do that so often in my life. It's hard to obey someone you don't trust. Something inside of me used to naturally want to buck up and not obey just to prove some kind of point. But that resistance to obedience was impulsive and driven by hurt, anger, sin, and whatever else was broken and hurting inside me. It was not driven by me wanting to choose the best life for myself.

The second reason obedience was hard for me was that I felt I was not able to follow through on the things I thought God had for me to do. I removed the relational process and saw God as a commander. I went to church and all the youth groups throughout my teen years and would go to the altar, cry crocodile tears, and within months or even days be back where I started. It was a hamster wheel I didn't know how to get off, because I did not have the relationship with Christ to be what sustained me and kept me from guilt and shame. I knew enough to know I was in sin and wasn't doing what God had for me, but I had no idea how to break the cycle. In the end, that only created shame, which caused me to want to hide from God. I was miserable.

Those were the biggest things that kept me back from all God had for me through obedience. What are those things for you? For some of us, the devil tries to make us believe that if we obey God, we will be stifled and life will be no fun. But when I read God's Word, I see that obedience is a doorway to success and joy.

Any time God asked someone to lay something down, walk away, or give something up, he always gave them something so much bigger and better in return. Amazing! He's asking us to give Him our junk and worthless possessions in return for Heavenly treasures. In Jeremiah 29:11, we read that God has plans to prosper us and not to harm us, to give us hope and a future. So obedience is a way of obtaining the good plans, future and hope he has for us. As we journey down that road with him, we get the pleasure of seeing that play out in our lives.

Obedience is also the ability to walk in power and authority. In 2 Corinthians 5:20, the Bible says that we are ambassadors for Christ. That is an extremely powerful word that Paul uses, and should not be taken lightly. When we become part of the Kingdom of God we are given authority to act on the King's behalf. He has bigger and better plans for us than we could ever imagine! Our Father and King has our best interest at heart. He knows exactly how he designed and built us and how we fit into his purpose with our lives. We will never truly be fulfilled in life if we don't lay down our agenda. Obedience to our Father allows us to have real authority in life and have His peace.

So, if obedience is a good life, what happens when we choose not to obey God? Essentially, what we are saying to Him and ourselves is we don't want what's best for us and His purpose for our lives. When we do that, we walk away from His protective covering over our lives, we give up part of our identity that will fulfill us, and we give up the blessing He has for us. God's provision is always there for His children when we walk in His will for our lives. I think our natural mind (our flesh) wants to think it's about control, and it's not. The truth is He knows what is best, because He loves us and created us to be how we are.

Disobedience Has Consequences, Not Punishment

Think of it this way—at any point, my kids could choose to disobey me and Kasey. They could rebel and decide not to listen to us. Now, it wouldn't make sense since we love them and care for them, but they have free will. Kasey and I would go to all means necessary to talk some sense into them, but at the end of the day, they have free will. Now, they could say they don't want to be part of the family, but the fact would never change they will always be our kids. Our love wouldn't change, but their choice would separate or cause division in our relationship. The consequence of that action would be they would no longer have the protection and provision we provide them in our home.

Even wanting to serve God and love Him, I have fallen short in the area of obedience. At one point, I took on a business partner because our business was expanding so fast and there was so much opportunity that I overlooked very obvious signs. There were so many times I sat down with this guy and just didn't have a good feeling. The Holy Spirit was showing me something wasn't right, and my stomach hurt. It was like having butterflies before an event. But I really needed the help and support and a business partner. As it turned out, the guy I was dealing with was a crook and had very bad intentions. Over the course of dealing with this guy for months, He essentially was able to lie his way through a contract, and we lost our million-dollar company overnight. We were devastated. Had I listened to Holy Spirit in my life, that would have turned out much different. I could have prospered had I embraced God's good plans for me, had I only listened.

Sometimes I have had great intentions, but sometimes I have been blind to the truth of what was driving me. See, sometimes we may disobey intentionally, but other times, we might disobey simply by not partnering with God and making decisions out of a partnership or relationship. I was very ambitious when I was young, and to some degree I still am (but much more cautious). We can easily mistake our greed for ambition. I had a phrase for years when I was young—I would say, "I open as many doors as I can and the ones God doesn't want me to go through He will close." I was using Scripture to back up my actions, so I thought it was all good.

Now, that was a time the Father was very gracious, and He did allow me to do that. If you were to look at my spiritual walk like a child growing up, I was a child spiritually. Several years down the road and ten years into my relationship with God, that started to change. He wanted to be a part of my decisions and walk me through them. At times I let Him, but I was still chasing that carrot in front of me. I knew my gift was in business, and I wanted to prove myself and makes lots of money. At one point I remember I had "doors" open all over the place and I had spread myself too thin. I remember asking God to shut doors for me and Him telling me "You need to close them." I was thinking, are you serious? This wasn't the deal, I opened them and you close them.

What the Father was teaching me was responsibility. I had to deal with the actions He never intended me to deal with. Had I followed His promptings or asked Him, I wouldn't have gotten myself into these messes. As I write this I think to myself—this is so basic, right? Why would anyone do that? And maybe you're thinking that yourself, but the problem is, I see it all the time from mature Christians. The Father allows us to grow in Him and make mistakes, that's all part of the process. But at some point, we have to decide to lay our giftings at His feet and allow Him to direct us. We think (or maybe I just did) that we are losing something, but we never are. The truth is we are allowing them to die so He can give them life and we can live more abundantly.

I believe, at its core, the cause of our disobedience is the fall of man. We have inherited Adam and Eve's poor decision to not trust the Father and believe a lie that was planted by Lucifer (the Father of Lies). The good news is that Jesus restored us back into the Father, but again it comes back to a choice. Do we chose to believe that our sins our forgiven, that we have been made new, and that we are loved? Our minds are being renewed as we spend time with the Father and read the

Word. It's a process, and we all fight it naturally. Obedience is hard when we don't know or spend time with the one asking us to do something. There is a hard balance, because at some point we have to step out in faith and allow God to show us His faithfulness when He asks us to do something. Over time, it gets much easier because He constantly shows Himself faithful and true.

If God isn't providing for us or things just "don't seem to be working out," there's a good chance we aren't walking the path He paved for us. If there's one thing that remains true that I have heard many times over the years, it is "go where the peace is." The Holy Spirit leads us in truth and peace—he peace that comes from Him only, and that is deep inside. We can be in situations that feel chaotic and crazy on the outside, but there can be peace within us that only He can give, and that's where we need to, and want to be.

Luke 11:28 says, "Blessed rather are those who hear the word of God and obey it." (NIV) And the Bible is full of examples of a good life that comes from obedience. One of my favorite stories is of Abraham and Sarah. God gave Abraham a promise and put that into his heart. The promise was that he would have a son. The problem was they were very old, and decades past child-birthing years. Abraham believed God and so did Sarah, but they got ahead of themselves and tried to make the promise happen themselves instead of God doing it in His perfect time. Sarah ended up having Abraham sleep with her maidservant to have a child as her own. They ended up having a child and naming him Ishmael. This caused an enormous amount of grief for Sarah and Abraham, because even though it sounded like a promise of God, it wasn't what He had in mind for them. He wanted them to have a child of their own through Sarah. He wanted to do the impossible through her, and he did, and she gave birth to Isaac.

81

I have found that usually, the dreams God gives us are way beyond what we can accomplish, as they should be. He wants to be in the equation because His desire is to be with us, and create with us. Had they waited, they would have saved years of grief in their lives and generations of pain and sorrow for people after.

The obedience continues when God tells Abraham to sacrifice his promised son, Isaac. Abraham takes Isaac to the mountaintop. This shows Abraham's heart and willingness to lay down his gift and promise from God. I have no doubts that Abraham was scared or had some doubts in the back of his mind, but He had to believe God was going to do something. God's promise to Abraham was that he would be the Father of nations. Now let's just think about this a little bit. You can't be a Father of Nations if you kill the thing that's going to fulfill that promise. By all means, it didn't make sense, and I believe Abraham had the faith to believe in something greater. What's most important in this story is that Abraham was willing to give up the very thing He was promised. Because of his faithfulness and obedience, we will always know him as the Father of faith.

When I read the Bible I read the biggest love story ever written. It is full of story after story of God pleading with Humanity to restore a broken relationship. The Bible is stories of people like you and me that are full of doubt, fear, anger and so much more. These stories show us it's okay to be broken or to fall down, it's just not okay to stay that way. His Word is there to give us hope and the strength to conquer what's in front of us. God wants to take what is broken in our lives and make it beautiful. I encourage you today, if you're walking in doubt or fear, pick up your Bible and read a story about Abraham, David, Ester or so many others. God shows up in all of their lives in a powerful way and forever changes them.

The story of Abraham certainly impacted me throughout my life! When we were young in the Lord, someone told us they thought God was saying that our lives would look much like the lives of Abraham and Sarah. We knew they were not talking about not having kids, because we already had a child. I liked the fact that Abraham was wealthy, so naturally as a businessman, I wanted to go with that. I'm still holding on to that one by faith. I mean that with some humor, so don't get religious on me and start judging now.

What Kasey and I realized was that it was about stepping out in faith and leaving everything we knew behind. Our families were no longer close by, and He was asking us to blindly follow Him. We didn't have mentors, family, or anyone else to help us. We were broke, had two businesses we were trying to learn how to run, and one child with another on the way.

It was like a good game of poker I like to watch on TV. We had a terrible hand, but we put in all our chips and said "all in." What's funny is on TV, as the viewer, you get to watch and you know who has what and if they are bluffing or not. God knew we had nothing but we were serious. Our nothing didn't concern Him—it was our action to lay it all down that He needed to allow Heaven's authority to step into our lives. God had a better hand and yet we still won, That's what makes Him an amazing Father.

I think of obedience as alignment. When we decide to make that step into obedience, what we are really doing is stepping into the authority that God has given us and placed on us. We now have the right to act on our Father's behalf with His full backing.

Earlier in the book, I brought up the story of Moses leading the people out of Egypt. During that process, there was so much obedience necessary from Moses for that all to take place. Had Moses not obeyed, who knows how long that whole process would have been delayed. I say delayed because I do believe God could have found someone else. There's always someone willing to take our place if we choose to disobey. It's not like we are the savior. Because Moses chose to obey God, he saw signs and wonders that had never been recorded and possibly had never happened before. Moses obeyed God, and it allowed what some scholars believe to be millions of people to be delivered from the hands of the Pharaoh. Obedience was the key ingredient that allowed Moses to step into his purpose and most importantly step into the authority that God had for him.

How Do We Know What God Is Asking Us to Do?

One of the biggest obstacles we have to obedience is that sometimes, it doesn't feel like God speaks clearly. So how do we know? For me personally, every time God has asked me to do something, it usually goes against my natural mind. It's contrary to what I think I want to do, and it is hard. If you look through scripture, I think you can find that to be true as well. It didn't make sense for Abraham to leave his family and country to go find another. Moses wasn't planning to lead a nation out of Egypt. David was only a boy and an outlaw running from the king. Jonah had to get swallowed by a whale before God got his attention, and when He decided to obey, a city was saved. In story after story, as we read the Bible, we read about people who step out in faith contrary to what they think makes sense, and God rewards them by showing up in powerful ways.

Sometimes we hear the still-small voice that leads us, but we have to fight our natural mind. Other times it can be a scripture that leaps off the pages at us and speaks to us, or a "gut instinct," or a doorway that God has opened up for us to step through. There's not just one way for God to speak to us, and sometimes that can be hard. But this is why building our relationship and spending time with God is important. To put it another way, my wife can speak with a look, or with words, or with body language, or many other ways. The only reason I know what her look means is because I have spent so much time with her and pursued trying to understand. We can be trying to listen to a voice when He's opening a door, and we will miss it. We need to pay attention and reflect on what's going on around us. God is always up to something in our lives, we just have to be paying attention and pursuing Him relationally.

Sometimes, we do hear it wrong, though. And what is our next step when we try to obey, but make a mistake? I think a big part of it is simply staying humble, continuing to pursue our good God, and not beating ourselves up. When I was in my early twenties, there was this beautiful piece of land I wanted to buy outside our city. There were beautiful mountains all around it, and where I wanted to build a home had a view that was amazing. At the time I was just learning to hear God's voice in my life and I had many friends who were learning this as well. I remember thinking that God wanted to give me this land, but instead of recognizing it as my thought, I might have even said "Thus saith the Lord."

After a couple phone calls and some deal-making, I ended up with the property and on some really good terms. Everything about the deal seemed like a blessing, and I was really excited. It was going to be a long-term hold, and I knew within a couple years I could sell half of what I bought for two to three times what I paid for all of it and keep the other half. But, not too many years after that was the 2007 crash, and we lost several properties including that one.

As I look back, there are several ways I can look at this. One is that all the proceeds I was paying were going to a church. The lady I bought it from was giving 100 percent to a church to bless them. Maybe at the time the church needed it, or maybe it went to someone who did. There are limitless ideas about what might have happened and how God might have had done much more than what I thought on the surface, and buying it, even losing it, helped someone in some way.

The other possibility is that I totally missed God and was going after something I wanted. To me, this makes the most sense, because I am not sure I really did get a word from God. I might never know. The point is, at times we are going to be wrong, or we will not see if we are right, and that's all part of the journey. The most important part is we keep trying with a willing and pure heart. It is the same with any relationship with a friend—at times there will be misunderstandings, but that doesn't mean we should throw our friendship out and not keep trying to understand!

At some point you have to decide that the risk if you don't obey is greater than the risk if you try to obey and don't hear it right. You have to ask yourself if not getting what God has for you is worth sitting in the same situation you are in. Fear will always cripple you and never empower you. Its purpose is to steal your authority and take power away. When you sense that or feel it coming, ask The Father to give you strength and courage, then step out and beat fear with a spiritual bat. Keep swinging till you hit fear out of the park!

Hearing God is part of how we grow as his children. When my children were little and learning to walk, I wouldn't have yelled at them or spanked them for falling while they were trying. That would be cruel and harmful. Instead we encouraged them and helped them as much as we could. How much more does our heavenly Father help and encourage us when He's your and my biggest champion, cheering us on?

Sometimes, God will speak to others around us, to help us hear from Him. My wife and I recently went through a situation at work that was really difficult. We knew God was speaking to us to do something and it took longer than it should have to do it. Because it took so long, it involved many late-night conversations that weren't very fun. There was and still is some healing that needs to take place.

During this journey of several months, there were a couple of people who gave us Biblical wisdom and direction. It was stuff we already knew, but we needed to hear it again. (Or maybe I just needed to hear it, not my wife, haha.) I think for her it was just an "I told you so" moment. She would never say that, but God was saying to me, "Listen to your wife." Having and allowing Godly people to speak into our life helped us obey and speed up the process to do what needed to be done. When we did, circumstances shifted for us and doors started to open up that were unexpected.

I know from experience that obedience is hard. Our flesh never wants to serve God. Our flesh wants to do what it wants and desires, and it's constantly fighting against our spirit. If we choose to walk in disobedience, we are laying down our power, authority and potential at Satan's feet and allowing him to dictate our lives. Just look back to Genesis and you see how disobedience wreaked havoc on Adam and Eve, who had the perfect lives up until that point. At the end of every podcast on *Are You Real*, I ask my guests to leave one piece of parting advice for my audience. I think If I was interviewing Adam or Eve they would say, without a doubt in my mind, "Obey God."

I want to end this chapter with an example of one of the first, and still one of the most profound times I obeyed the word of God, and the consequences that played out after. The first time I ever really stepped out in faith and obeyed God was when I got married. Kasey was competing in pageants and I was playing football on a scholarship at the time. Kasey had won a local pageant and competed in the Ms. New Mexico competition and won the Talent part that year. She was only a freshman at the time and a senior whom she was friends with had won. Things were looking very promising for her to win the next year. She had everything she needed to go all the way. I was playing football on a scholarship and was planning on going to Europe or wherever else I could go. I wanted to take it as far as I could. Kasey and I were living together at the time and had all our bills paid for. We were getting support from people mostly because of Kasey and her potential to win Ms. New Mexico the next year. We started going to church together around this time and started to seek the Lord again.

At different times, both Kasey and I heard God say to get married or separate. I will never forget Kasey and I having a sit down and having to tell each other what we heard. I can't remember who told who first but we had both heard the same thing and felt the need to share. We felt like we were between a rock and a hard place. In our minds and the world's eyes, we had so much to lose. First I'm pretty sure there is no *Mrs.* New Mexico pageant to compete in. Kasey would have to do more than just give up her title—we were going to lose our financial help and support. I could still keep playing football, but we weren't going to have any help to live and we had no idea what to do.

Marriage to us wasn't really an option, but we knew we had to be "all in" with God one way or another. After a series of many events and things getting in the way of us marrying, one day we went to the court house, filled out our paperwork, and called our pastor. We showed up at his office on Kasey's lunch break and we got married. This truly was a no-looking-back moment for us. It was like the Israelites leaving Egypt and going to a promised land when they had no idea what it looked like. We were stepping out in faith completely blind. And yet, I think if we did not obey God, what might have happened? Would we have missed important things, moments together and experiences? Yes! I am forever thankful I listened to God.

That is my best example of what obedience looks like in our walk with God. It's scary, and most of the time it costs us something. At this point in our life, it cost us everything. But I can tell you this—the price you think you are going to pay doesn't come close to the treasure and reward He has for you in return. I hope these stories and thoughts have helped to reshape and inspire you to think of obedience to God as the biggest asset in your life instead of something God does to try to control you or take away your power.

Obedience is vital if we want a transformed life. But I know that for me (and probably you) one of the biggest barriers to obedience is, in the end, fear. Fear of being controlled, fear of getting it wrong, fear of losing something. In the next chapter, I want to take you on a journey to learn how I address fears and seek to understand and disempower any fear that would get in the way of my obedience to God.

Transforming Steps:

1. What feelings come up when you think of obedience? Do you think of punishment or fear? Do you think of control? Continue to reframe obedience to God in terms of the gifts and possibilities that are in it!
2. Think of a time you did not obey what you thought God was telling you. What were the consequences for you? How can you avoid falling into the same thing again?
3. Think of a time you obeyed God. What was the fruit of that obedience in your life?

Chapter Six

OVERCOMING FEAR WITH GOD'S WORD

"I don't know about you, but I would say the number one thing, for me, that gets in the way of my obedience and willingness to speak and see transformation in my life is fear. As I mentioned in the first chapter, maybe you believe that words are powerful, but you have areas of fear, mindsets or reservations when it comes to actually speaking them out. If you have tried to speak life and given up, or if you have felt these areas are not able to change (or worse, were intended by God to not flourish) it is time to examine your fears and mindsets and see where the disconnection is taking place. Only then can you become connected to God again in that area. I want to encourage you here. Often, if you want some area of your life to transform, it is because God Himself is the one that put that on your heart! He wants it to transform as well, and He is on your team!

The Problem of Fear: Faulty Mindsets

I know from experience that our faulty mindsets can create major roadblocks. I have been there, too, and I experience that in new areas all the time. It is an important next step to recognize and address our fears and mindsets before continuing on our journey. Why? Because bad mindsets, including ones based in fear, are the main thing that will keep us from speaking out words that will align us with the word of God.

In the first chapter, I wrote about how hesitant I was to speak out what God put in my heart about my finances. I was afraid to feel like a crazy person and I was afraid of being greedy. None of the things that stopped me were from God. They were fear-based. The fears were empowered by faulty mindsets and thought patterns. These mindsets kept me from truth. Had I not had these strongholds in my mind and thoughts, I might have spoken over my finances and started living the life God had for me years before.

Fear will often stop us from God's best and keep us from speaking and hearing His words. It is a powerful force in opposition of God. It is the enemy of faith. Anywhere you are not operating in faith, you will probably find some fear strongholds operating to keep you in fear. There are no fears in our lives besides the fear of God, so if you are feeling fear, that is a good place to start inviting God in.

How do you recognize negative thoughts and fears? You simply pay attention to your thoughts and words! Fear and faithless mindsets start in the heart, and work their way outward through our words. We will not have long-term success changing our words if we do not change our hearts. These two things play off of each other in a terrible way. As you speak death, the good God has for you is defiled, as you see it is defiled it feels bad and hopeless, and then you are discouraged and you speak death.

Matthew 15:11 says, "What goes into someone's mouth does not defile them, but what comes out of their mouth, that is what defiles them." (NIV) We need to start with the heart because that is where the transformation starts. It is only then that we can get to the root of why words are not having the power they can have in your life. It is important to dig deep and examine what is in our hearts that is holding us back from using our words powerfully. In this chapter, I want to show you my journey as a kind of model for you to follow as you start to think about your own fears.

This is not a book about finances, but this book includes finances because that has been my biggest area of fear and biggest area where I needed to grow in trusting God. Because my heart struggles to trust God in finances, I struggle to speak God's words over finances. I have had to dig deep to think about why I did not truly believe God cared about my finances and wanted me to be successful. I realized there were a lot of faulty mindsets that had come from the church, or my past, and did not come from God. Thought patterns and fears are usually created through our environment growing up, so it often takes some work to recognize them. But once you do recognize them, you can gain a whole new level of freedom.

Overcoming Faulty Mindsets

As my journey continued from that moment where God told me to speak over my finances, I realized that if I was going to continue to speak life, some old thoughts would have to go. It is much easier to deal with these things when you are able to break your thoughts into smaller pieces and think about each part separately. In the next few pages, I want to break these thoughts down to give you an example of what you can do in your own life to partner with God to become free and feel released to speak words of transformation over your life. Remember, everything, even your freedom, is co-created! You have to play an active part! God does not see us as damsels in distress, He sees us as heirs to His power and authority.

In my story, the first thought pattern that I had to release was the idea that money was a taboo subject with God. I had a mindset that I should not directly ask God to make my finances prosper, or ask Him what to do when I was financially struggling. Why did I think it was a bad idea to talk about money with God? I think money has been a taboo subject with people for a long time. Growing up, and especially in church, we are often afraid to talk about money because it is a loaded topic. Most people have very strong thoughts about money. From how to earn it, to how to spend it, to investing and saving, to feelings of anger that people misuse money, and on and on. Most people become emotionally triggered when it comes to money. Most tend to allow their emotions to dictate how they feel. The result is that people tend to avoid talking about money to keep from emotionally triggering themselves or others. Did you know the things we fear to talk about with other people are not things we need to fear to talk about with God? I do not think God is triggered by money, or politics, or any other area that is difficult for humans to discuss. Once I realized this, I was a step closer to trusting that I could talk with God and feel safe and open about my financial situation. Let's be honest, if this did not change, I would not have felt comfortable continuing to speak over my finances.

The second problematic mindset was that I was afraid of being greedy. This was one of my biggest fears. Throughout history, some have considered it honorable to be a Christian who is poor. The church has a long history of idolizing poverty and self-inflicted lack, which I believe is demonic and not biblical. Nowhere does it say in the Bible that we should purposefully cause ourselves to suffer. All it says is that when suffering comes, we do our best to deal with it in a way that honors God. The poverty mindset hinders us and our relationships. Who can feel God's peace and sufficiency when they constantly are prideful about their lack and make lack the God they focus on and worship? Who can put attention toward relationships when they are cold, sleepless and starving because of prideful, self-imposed lack God did not ordain? If we are broke, we are not our best selves. We become beggars. I realized if we are always living in a state of lack, the world will see Christians as needy beggars. How much more powerful am I if I can offer the world help though the abundance I have? How much better for the outside world to see who God really is! He is a God who provides!

Greed is something to be aware of, but if my fear of greed was so strong it could keep me from doing what God asked me to do, the fear of greed had to go! I think the best way is to be unattached to money either way. Like God, to not feel emotionally attached to it. I think we have the wrong perspective, because we have not looked at money properly: as a tool God has allowed us to use. Fearing money can be an idol just as much as greed itself can be an idol. Anything that keeps us from God's words and inhibits our connection with Him is an idol. These new thoughts were helpful for me to release this stronghold in my mind.

The third bad mindset I had was that I felt awkward talking out loud in a way that made me feel I was talking to myself, or to an inanimate object (my money). In our culture, most of the people that we see talking to themselves or objects have mental health issues, and I did not want to feel I was emulating someone who was mentally and emotionally struggling for no reason. Yet, this was just a perception. Prayer, in a sense, often looks the same as speaking to oneself, and Jesus Himself did this when He prayed to the Father! In addition, if we believe our words do create our reality, then we need to act like it even if others do not have this revelation yet. Really what this boiled down to was my ego and pride. I did not want anyone to think poorly of me, and I wanted to think highly of myself. The sobering truth was that this pride was part of what was keeping me in the lack that I was not proud of!

Lastly, I feared I was not enough and would never have enough. I believed that God did not think I deserved to prosper, or couldn't help me prosper. When I reflected on this, I think these thoughts started when I grew up in a home where there was much lack. I had a father in the natural world who loved me and gave me so much in many ways. He was not my biological dad, but he loved me tremendously. Despite that, there were many pulls for money and not a lot of income in our family. There was nothing wrong with how I grew up, but I personally created a sense of myself that was centered around the idea that I was always lacking. I thought that was who I truly was.

When I say we had lack, I mean my family was so poor after my brother died that we had to take cold showers in the winter one year. We had very little heat in the house throughout one winter—it was a horrible experience. Growing up, if I wanted anything, I had to work really, really hard to get it. Meanwhile, I saw some of my friends simply ask their parents, and their parents would give them things. Me? I had to work for it. I carried this into my relationship with God. I didn't believe asking and speaking things out would get me what I asked for in terms of material things, because it did not work like that at home. This made me think I would always be the kind of person who "would have to work for it." And also the kind of person who would never have enough. All this made it very hard for me to trust God in this area.

So those were the mindsets holding me back that were based in fear. And the result of these mindsets let me see that in my heart, I was fighting God. I was constantly speaking over my finances things that were not true and were actually getting me further away from God's plan! I was co-creating with the enemy. I certainly was not my best self. Sometimes I would spiral into such deep fear that I would need my wife to help me see that things were not all doom-and-gloom. I am thankful she was there, but I was not proud of bringing that to our relationship, and now know I would not have had to do that if it were not for my mindsets and fears.

God's Words Transform Fear to Faith

Which areas do you feel weak in when it comes to speaking God's truth into your life? Fear of anything other than God will not bring healthy transformation into our lives. Fear is the opposite of faith, and every time we fear, we walk the opposite way of God. In fear, we cannot experience the fullness of God. In this chapter so far, I have demonstrated there can be bad spiritual mindsets, such as "God doesn't want this for me," faulty mindsets learned from family history, such as "It's always been this way for me/us," or faulty mindsets learned from church, such as "If you keep any money you are greedy, you should give it away." Finally, there are bad mindsets that come from our own ego, one of mine being, "I don't want to feel silly."

Mark 3:25 says, "If a house is divided against itself, that house cannot stand." (NIV) When our heart is divided with fear and doubt, we cannot walk into the transformation God has for us. It is worth our time to identify these things and ask God to co-create with us in a way that uproots them from our hearts.

We are called to constantly transform into the image of God and think how He thinks (see 2 Corinthians 3:18; Romans 8:29 Romans 12:2). Once we have identified our fear and strongholds, we have to be aggressive about countering those arguments with two things: truth and faith!

In 2 Corinthians 10:5, we read, "We demolish arguments and every pretension that sets itself up against the knowledge of God, and we take captive every thought to make it obedient to Christ." (NIV) Let's start to demolish the things holding us back from using our words to create transformation and growth!

One of the best ways to learn what is the truth, and start to increase our faith, is to spend time with God and in God's Word. Psalm 34:4 says, "I sought the LORD, and he answered me; he delivered me from all my fears" (NIV). Romans 10:17 says, "So faith comes from hearing, and hearing through the word of Christ" (ESV). So, the next big step toward transformation is to research what God says about the area that we are seeking to transform. This gives us power and spiritual ammunition to align our words with God.

Acts 17:11 says, "Now the Berean Jews were of more noble character than those in Thessalonica, for they received the message with great eagerness and examined the Scriptures every day to see if what Paul said was true." (NIV) What might happen in your heart if you eagerly examined the scriptures to see what God has to say about the area where you struggle to speak life? What would happen if you allow God to come in with His Word and help show you how to speak?

When I started to search the scriptures, it was interesting to me to try to identify how God felt about money. As mentioned above, I realized that money was not a triggering topic to Him. But I also realized it is something He has given to us as a tool. When I go into my workshop, I don't look at a certain tool and feel emotional things when I look at it. It is just a tool to make life easier, though if misused, it will make life harder! Money is not dangerous, bad and detrimental, but it becomes that way if our heart is in a bad place. In the same way a hammer is not a bad tool, but it can be detrimental if it is used with anger, destruction or carelessness. It can also feel unhelpful if we have never thought about how to use it correctly!

The first commandment is to love the Lord our God with all our heart. If we put fear first, we will be in trouble. If we put money first, we will be like the tax collectors in the Bible who were willing to hurt and oppress people for financial gain. If we put God first, we will value relationships with God and others more than money. This is why God financially blessed Solomon when Solomon asked for wisdom instead of riches (1 Kings 3). God saw his priorities to God and others were right—he wanted wisdom more than money.

As I re-read the scriptures, I realized they did not always say what I thought they said. There are many scriptures that speak about wisely stewarding money, using money to care for your family, and always having something to give to others in need. All of which you cannot do without money. One passage that is often misinterpreted is 1 Timothy 6:10-11. Paul says, "For the love of money is a root of all kinds of evil. Some people, eager for money, have wandered from the faith and pierced themselves with many griefs. But you, man of God, flee from all this, and pursue righteousness, godliness, faith, love, endurance and gentleness." (NIV) Somehow, either in pop culture or the church, this verse is believed to say, "Money is the root of all evil." But God did not say that. In fact, in this passage, Paul distinctly says it is the LOVE of money that causes you to wander from faith and is the root of evil. I had to realize that idolizing and loving money above God is very different from prospering financially and seeing that bring you closer to God and into deeper faith.

It is clear in scripture that someone cannot love God and money (Matthew 6:24). Matthew 6:25 says we should not worry about our food and clothes. Some Christians, I believe, have mistakenly taken this to mean, "Don't ever think about it or talk about it." But there is a big difference between thinking while trusting God, and choosing to worry about it. If I see money as a tool, I will not worry about it. I will simply realize it is there and think about the best way to use it, given my situation. God does not want money to trigger fear for us!

Another verse that I found I had misinterpreted was Hebrews 13:5. This says, "Keep your lives free from the love of money and be content with what you have, because God has said, 'Never will I leave you; never will I forsake you.'" Again, we see that God does not say "Keep your lives free from money." He says the LOVE of money. Why? Because we can't love God and money. We are told to be content in knowing God is with us and will provide for us. Money is not our provider. God is. It doesn't matter if you are wealthy, prosperous, or just making it, money will not save you, but God can. That is the point of this passage—it does not say to keep our lives free from money.

In Matthew 25:14-30, Jesus talks about money, and while He is using it as a metaphor for the kingdom, I do think He expects us to take what we have in every area and multiply it for the benefit of His kingdom. My dad always taught me that when you borrow something, you give it back in better shape than you got it. I am thankful for that lesson because it helps me understand the scriptures. When the master gave the servants money, the one who buried it was called wicked, but the ones who increased it were called faithful! Our heart toward money needs to be: What do you want me to do with the money I have, and how can I be a good steward and increase it?

Of course, the most glaring evidence that God is not against prosperity and wealth is found in many of the lives of those who fathered our faith. I had somehow forgotten that Abraham and David lived lives of financial prosperity beyond what we could imagine! David was called by God himself "a man after God's own Heart." Job was described as the wealthiest man in the world at the time. God said of

Job, "There is no one on earth like him; he is blameless and upright, a man who fears God and shuns evil." I don't think it was ever about money for these men. They pursued God, and loved God, and wealth simply followed them! Esther is another good example of this. In the New Testament, God used wealthy Wise Men to bring gifts to Jesus. Joseph of Arimathea is described in Matthew as a rich man. He donated his tomb to Jesus. In Matthew 8, a wealthy centurion paid for a synagogue to be built.

After a critical examination of scripture, I felt reassured that wealth was not a bad thing to ask for, but it was a bad thing to ask for if my heart was in the wrong place. When I am building something, is not bad to ask for a certain tool if the tool will help me achieve my goal. It is bad if I start to worship the tool! I became more convinced that if I did not speak God's truth over my finances, my fears would end up leading me away from God! My finances would be put above God, then. This increased my faith and confidence to continue to speak to my finances, and to believe that it was God whowanted me to prosper as I pursued relationship with Him.

Isn't God's written Word amazing? Talk about transformative power! Maybe finances are not an area where you struggle, and maybe you already knew all this. But what I want to demonstrate to you is a process. Whenever you are struggling to speak God's words over your life, I encourage you to go back to scripture and see what God has already said. If the words you heard are from God, they will also be in the Bible. He will confirm his Word to you!

Overcoming Fear Transforms Your Relationship With God

Now we come to my favorite part of the chapter. When God said to speak over my finances, I assumed it was because He wanted my finances to change. What I did not realize, however, was that He wanted to change so much more! The biggest lesson I learned through this whole journey facing my fears and bad mindsets is NOT that I should speak to increase my money. If that was it, this would be a very different book! The biggest lesson was that God loved me more than I ever knew possible and wanted me to walk in a deeper truth, wanted my heart to be transformed to think more like Him, and wanted a deeper relationship with me. Relationship has been my biggest reward, and that is the ultimate reward of speaking God's Word in our lives.

Reflecting now, this is the difference between speaking God's words, and the "name it, claim it" movement. The "name it, claim it" movement did not keep the focus where it should be: on relationship! The motivation to speak was not based in a relationship with God and others, so it was not from God's heart, and it was doomed to fail. It promoted independence from God. Choosing independence from God is the sin of Satan and the sin that leads to destruction. God himself is dependent on the Holy Spirit and Jesus to be able to accomplish his work. "Name it, claim It" doesn't work because it is a relationship with an idea of self-sufficiency through declaration, it is not based out of a loving, reciprocal, co-created relationship with God and a desire to see His kingdom flourish.

Everything in the world belongs to God. The only thing He cannot create on His own is your choices, your thoughts, your willingness to engage in transformation, and your love for Him. The most valuable things in life are the things we cannot have, or cannot get easily, things we have to pursue for a long time. The story of Jesus reminds us that God's heart is for us, to pursue us, and to have a relationship with us. God treasures us, because He has spent thousands of years pursuing us and pursuing humanity. He will not force a relationship with him, but He will not create it without your participation and cooperation. The thing He wants most of all is a relationship with you!

The fact that God spoke to me and expressed that He cared about my finances showed me He cared for me, wanted me to trust Him, and wanted me to participate to co-create my life and destiny as a partnership in relationship with Him. He wanted to step in and be my Father; to love me, to be my older brother, to teach me a better way. He wanted to provide me with enough to meet my needs. He wanted me to be released and be free to stop worrying. He wanted me to delight in Him as my provider. He wanted abundance for me in my relationship with Him, in areas where I felt powerless and discouraged on my own.

The result has been that pushing through my fears and speaking God's words healed some places in my heart and helped me to trust Him with more of my heart. He found a place inside me that needed some major remodeling, and He blessed me with that. He wanted to lovingly restore me to whom I was meant to be. He wants the same for you!

The result has also been that I finally feel free to enjoy the gifts and skills God has given me. The truth is, God made me to enjoy business and enjoy making money! I used to think it was not spiritual enough as a career. That God might prefer me to do something else. But through the process of realigning my finances to God's word, I realized a beautiful truth: there was nothing wrong with enjoying business and making money. In essence, there was nothing wrong with how God created me.

I was given freedom to use my gifts and talents in the area of business. I realized that this is how I minister to others, and have enough to give to support others. My friend Bob Hasson puts it well. He says, "God's ultimate destiny for business is that it empowers philanthropically minded men and women to make a positive difference in the world for Christ." Suddenly, I was empowered in a new way to pursue my calling, destiny and place in a way that would benefit the kingdom. I was empowered to speak words that declared and came into alignment with the destiny God has had for me all along. Really, it was never about money. I was about love, trust, and acceptance, and about inviting God further into my life.

God's Word is so life-giving to correct us! When our lives are transformed into what God has planned, we are free to think about and love others better. I cannot give what I do not have. I cannot give my children abundance if I do not have it. I cannot be as emotionally at peace when I live with fear of finances. I cannot encourage others to trust God for provision if I do not. I cannot provide as much provision to charities, churches or my employees if I am constantly facing lack.

The Father was wanting me to break fear over my spirit, over my life, and over my identity. Those areas were the areas where I had dry bones in my life. He wanted to break me of the habit of the negative things I was saying. I was able to see the power of my words in the area of my life. This allowed me to walk in a greater measure of my God-ordained destiny.

Some days, when something hard happens, I find myself going back to my old ways of speaking negative, or not speaking life over a situation. In those situations, sometimes it feels better to speak death. But the big motivator for me now is not the situation. I can finally see how speaking death hurts my relationships, my faith, my hope and my heart. Those are more valuable than a momentary release of death from my mouth.

My prayer for you is that through this chapter, you have been encouraged to see how your heart can be transformed to experience a new level of connection and relationship with God when you hear and speak His words, and reject the fear and strongholds that stop you! God wants to do things with your life—He wants to partner with you, He wants to bring forth your destiny, He wants to empower you to grow closer to Him and others! I hope this chapter has given you an understanding of how to partner with Him to remove fear from your life so you can fully speak out and align with what He has for you in His heart.

Transforming Steps:

1. Spend a few minutes in prayer and ask God to help you to identify the root of what is holding you back from speaking His word. Remember, it might help to ask Him to help you explore spiritual strongholds, mindsets passed down from family and church history, and if your ego comes into play at all. Ask God what His perspective is on these strongholds and His opinion on how they are holding you back.
2. Search the scriptures to find verses on the topic that you are struggling with. Remember, your mouth speaks from the abundance of your heart. Ask God to transform and soften your heart to hear His Word and believe His Word in your heart.
3. Keep the focus on relationship. How would it impact your relationship with God if you were able to use His words to transform your life? How would this impact the people around you? If you do not think that the words will have a positive impact on your relationship with God and others, you might not be speaking God's words after all.

Chapter Seven

NATURAL AND SUPERNATURAL TRANSFORMATION

"As we consider how to be empowered to be connected to the source of life, and the words of God, we must consider that God's ways are not our ways. To us, one barrier is that things may not make sense. Even if we are trying to be obedient, and even if we are able to overcome our fear of speaking out God's words in our life, we will miss some of what He has for us if we are not able to consider the aspects of God that are mysterious to us, and that do not make sense to our natural mind.

Supernatural Powers, Natural People

I believe we were made to operate in a supernatural world where not everything is fully seen with our natural eyes. What do you think of when you think of the supernatural? When I think of it, my mind always goes to all the movies that have come out over the past couple years. I think of movies like *The Avengers* and all the other superhero movies. I am naturally attracted to these movies because of the action and the message behind them. It's usually a plot of good versus evil in some sense, and they are usually great parables that mirror stories and lessons from the Bible. I think most people may not see or be able to translate the "parable" because they don't know scripture or their Heavenly Father, who is the greatest storyteller of all time. But, the point is that when people see these movies, they say the characters are supernatural because they have gifts, behaviors and powers that "normal" people do not have.

Some people may not make this connection, but to me, this sounds an awful lot like the early Church. In the most basic form, having faith is a supernatural power. You are engaging in a supernatural activity when you invite Jesus to be your savior and when you are saved through grace. That is not a natural process. It is not like Jesus shows up in person, goes with you to dinner, and has you sign a physical contract, and then you are saved. It is another supernatural moment when we can love our enemy, engage in joy despite pain, or demonstrate God to the world through our actions. But there is more to the supernatural as well—1 Corinthians 12 tells us the following:

"Now about the gifts of the Spirit, brothers and sisters, I do not want you to be uninformed. You know that when you were pagans, somehow or other you were influenced and led astray to mute idols...There are different kinds of working, but in all of them and in everyone it is the same God at work.

Now to each one the manifestation of the Spirit is given for the common good. To one there is given through the Spirit a message of wisdom, to another a message of knowledge by means of the same Spirit, to another faith by the same Spirit, to another gifts of healing by that one Spirit, to another miraculous powers, to another prophecy, to another distinguishing between spirits, to another speaking in different kinds of tongues, and to still another the interpretation of tongues. All these are the work of one and the same Spirit, and he distributes them to each one, just as he determines."

Every Christian is told here that they have gifts given by the spirit of God that are not natural, but supernatural! Not only that, but when we read through the Bible, it is full of amazing stories that we can't wrap our minds around. If we can't make sense of it, then we put it in a box or category and call it "supernatural." I don't think as believers that was supposed to ever be the case. I think what we call the supernatural is, in actuality, God's natural.

The Problem With Disconnecting Ourselves

Big problems come when we allow the "natural" and "supernatural" to be separated. If we separate our natural from God's natural, we no longer have the mind of Christ toward a situation. We are essentially separating God and putting Him in a box.

Many years ago, I was doing a painting job for a man whom I went to church with. He had been there for several years and seemed to be fairly grounded in the Word. When he was given his original bid for the paint job we had agreed on two colors in the house and painting his trim. When we went to start, he changed his mind and had us paint almost every room a different color, and we ended up with seven to nine different colors throughout the house. We told him there would be an upcharge and were very upfront with him about it and he agreed, but once we finished, he refused to pay. We had several rounds of conversations and I finally asked him, "As a Christian, how can you justify your actions when the Bible says not to steal? You have stolen labor and materials you are not paying for, and you lied about your commitment to pay for it."

This man went on to tell me that church was church and business was business. The truth is there is no separation. The man had created the separation to justify His lack of right living. But, I believe that who we are and what we believe

107

carries over into all areas of our lives. If Jesus is our foundation and our rock, then His beliefs, His character, His nature is ours. I have compassion for this man, because his beliefs were twisted. He had separated something in his mind that was never supposed to be separated. He did it for his own gain and comfort, but my company and team were cheated and had to take the consequences of his lack of connection between the two worlds he'd created.

I believe this is what many people have done with the power of God. We have separated His power into either stories in the Bible or into something we think of as only for those who have "extra faith or abilities." This isn't like the Marvel movies where there's only a couple "super Christians." We all have access to God's natural "supernatural." When we walk with him and spend time with Him, His character, beliefs and nature start to overflow into our lives and those around us. It's after we start to spend time with him that His supernatural starts to flow through us and into others' lives!

So what gets in the way of us claiming our supernatural gifts and walking with God's spirit? If it is so good, why does it sometimes feel hard and awkward and even scary? Well, Satan knew in the garden that pride and self-will would cause separation. He knew firsthand because he had experienced it.

Isaiah 14:13-14 says of Satan that,

"You said in your heart,
"I will ascend to the heavens;
I will raise my throne
above the stars of God;
I will sit enthroned on the mount of assembly,
on the utmost heights of Mount Zaphon.
I will ascend above the tops of the clouds;
I will make myself like the Most High."

Satan decided he wanted to be like God and try to exalt himself. Because of his actions, he was kicked out of Heaven and has raised havoc on Earth ever since. Satan comes into our lives and constantly lies to us to get us to not believe what the Father has said about us or to us. The supernatural reminds us we do not know it all, and that we're not God. Just look at what happened in the Garden. Satan was able to get Eve to doubt God's goodness and to think she knew better than God, and she sinned. Like Satan, Eve was kicked out. She was disconnected from the power source. Satan knows if he can get us to disobey or do things on our own that we will mess them up, or lose power.

On a recent project, a homeowner decided he wanted to change out all the wall plugs in the house. He wanted to do it to save money, because having a licensed electrician was cost-prohibitive. After he decided to change out all the plugs, only a couple places in the house worked, and it was causing problems. At first he tried to blame us as a company for doing something to the house, but when the professional electrician showed up and did a little investigation, they found he had hooked up all the plugs wrong. They looked right on the outside, but behind the wall, the wires were wrong.

Our lives are much like this. We decide to not let the master electrician into our lives who designed us, and try and solve problems ourselves with our natural minds that can't see behind to the truth of what is really going on. The beauty of God is He steps into the situation and makes things right when we let him. He turns ashes into beauty. Isaiah 61:3 says that God will "provide for those who grieve in Zion—to bestow on them a crown of beauty instead of ashes, the oil of joy instead of mourning, and a garment of praise instead of a spirit of despair. They will be called oaks of righteousness, a planting of the LORD for the display of his splendor." (NIV)

Supernatural and natural are not separated for God. In fact, what we think is supernatural is very natural to Him. Healing, transformation, miracles; they are all part of the normal life of Jesus. He wants that power to come through us to transform the world around us. The Hoover Dam is an example that comes to mind when I think of how we are to let God's power flow through us. The dam itself is about as tall as a seventy-story skyscraper! It is 700 feet tall, 1,200 feet wide, and 660 feet thick at the base. The dam creates a lack that is filled with around ten trillion gallons of water.

The dam serves power to over a million people in its area and is a major blessing. If you think this is overstated, just take away power from all those people and see what happens. I think you would have complete chaos. I think we are much like this modern marvel. We are created to be a blessing and release God's power into the lives and situations around us through natural and supernatural means. When we connect to God, the ultimate "living water" at the source, we never have to worry about provision. He is all, in all, and can do anything that He desires. We just have to decide to turn on the breaker in all areas of our life and let Him flow.

With Power Comes Responsibility

I want to go back to the idea of superheroes in the movies. Usually, they start off somewhat unaware of their powers. As they become aware, they may have trouble understanding how or when to use the power, and they may try to run away out of fear of their gift. What I love about these movies is that, ultimately, the hero discovers, like Spiderman, that "With great power comes great responsibility." Yes, often at a personal cost or inconvenience, they are able to help and save others. What a picture of the Christian life with God!

Maybe you're reading this now and you are just discovering that supernatural gifts exist, or maybe you know they exist, but don't know how to practically take the next steps toward growth. In order to experience the supernatural, we must be in the presence of it. That can happen through being around someone who has a close walk with God. When I was younger, there were services that I went to that were life-changing for me because our pastor would take the time to cultivate an atmosphere for our Heavenly Father to be in. Sometimes, the services would last two to four hours. It sounds like a long time, but when God shows up and lives are being changed, it doesn't feel long.

What it did for me (and it should do for you) is to draw you in and whet your appetite for God and what is possible. It is kind of like going to the grocery store (you know, the big store you can't walk out of without spending hundreds of dollars on bulk stuff). You can walk out with a year's supply of popcorn or anything else if you want. When you walk around, they have free samples you can try. It's just enough to allow you to like it, but if you show up hungry, you're not getting enough to get full. God wants you to experience Him through others and learn about what is possible from others. But there is so much more to encounter when you walk with Him personally.

Nothing will compare with when you walk into Him. God doesn't fit in a box and never will. I do know that over the years, I've read and heard many times that we are the sum of the five people we are around the most or allow to influence our lives. If we are really after and pursuing God, then three of those spots are taken. We get the Father to nurture us, Jesus to walk with us through the word, and the Holy Spirit to lead us. When we have the three most influential beings walking through life with us, we can't help but be radically changed, with Heaven's supernatural power flowing around us.

Another way to begin to accept the supernatural power of God so we can see what is possible in a situation is with the Scriptures. Proverbs 3:5-6 says, "Trust in the Lord with all your heart and lean not on your own understanding; in all your ways submit to him, and he will make your paths straight." (NIV)

When our minds are set on things above (Colossians 3:2), then Heaven's economy becomes our supernatural bank. I don't just mean that financially, but in love, joy, peace, hope, and all the other things that God is the source of. We have access to anything we need in our heart, even when the world says it is not possible.

Pursue God in all you do and make His principles in your life a focus. The super is an overflow of what we see and hear in our quiet time with the Father. We need both. Jesus was not just supernatural. He was also shockingly natural. That is why some did not recognize Him as God. I love the fact the Jesus was both God and man. Had He come as just God, there would be no way for us to relate. We would (or at least I would) think there's no way to achieve or do what He did, but that's not the case. There's two really important things that come to my mind when I think of Jesus's life. First and foremost, Jesus imitated the Father, and that was our example.

In John 5:19-20, we read, "Jesus gave them this answer: "Very truly I tell you, the Son can do nothing by himself; he can do only what he sees his Father doing, because whatever the Father does the Son also does. For the Father loves the Son and shows him all he does. Yes, and he will show him even greater works than these, so that you will be amazed."

If this is what Jesus came to do, then why should we think any different? If we want to walk in power, then there's only one source, and that's our Heavenly Father. Jesus had authority because he walked in unity with what His Father was doing. The second important thing that ministers to me is that Jesus took time to rest. That might not be a big deal to some, but for me it's a huge struggle.

Let me just give you a recent example of my struggle. Just this past week, it was a Friday night and it was about 9 p.m. I was completely wiped out and exhausted for the week. Kasey came and lay with me on the couch as we watched T.V. She mentioned several times that we should go to bed because I looked tired. I was past that point because I was getting delirious and giggly. Every time she said we should go to bed, I would tell her to hush and put my finger on her mouth. I told her not to speak of such things. We would then laugh and she would say, "Oh, Jon."

I have a bad habit, and I've gotten much much better, but it's hard for me to miss out. I push myself harder and farther than I should at times. Rest is overlooked and so needed in this day and age. In fact, when we rest with God, it is supernatural, because we become more productive, which goes against natural laws. But usually, we are so caught up in our phones, TV, Netflix, and all the other technology grabbing for our attention.

Our minds are being bombarded with ideas, thoughts, and lies trying to tell us how and what to think. We need to take the time to rest and delight in what the Father is doing. I hear a friend of mine often say, we are human BEings, not human DOings. I have to learn and train myself not to always do. Jesus as a human took the time to rest, enjoy His friends around Him, and be present. Jesus was our example to follow—if He needed to rest, then so do we. Jesus was part God and part man, we are only 100% human. How much more do we need?

When the natural collides with the supernatural, we can expect amazing things to happen. One story of how this happened in our lives Kasey already shared in the third chapter. When she was a young girl, she had a step-dad who was abusive and caused issues that only God could heal. But, God healed Kasey's womb, supernaturally. It was never God's plan for her to get abused or wounded, but it was His plan and intention to turn those dead bones into life. God is the ultimate restorer. Mankind has destroyed and abused so many things, but His love for us continues to pursue us and restore things back to what He intended in natural and supernatural ways. Imagine if we had not been open to supernatural things—we would never have felt the fullness and redemption of God's love! We would have cut His love out because it didn't look like how we thought it should look. Instead, we stepped into the supernatural that night and it forever changed our lives. Kasey soon was pregnant with our first baby girl. We had two more kids all within eighteen months of each other, and we had a family! What the devil intended to use and destroy her life with now was giving birth to three amazing kids.

God's Supernatural Increases Love and Relationship

When God has shown up in our lives, there has never been any mistake about who did it. I would like to take credit at times and think I was smarter than I am, but the truth is I'm not. When God shows up, there is no mistake. I look all throughout the Bible, and I know God is the same yesterday, today, and forever. When He showed up for the Israelites and split the red sea, when he caused manna to fall from heaven, or water to come out of a rock. It's when we get in those places that God likes to show up and show off. It's like He can finally step in because we have no choice but to let Him. We are out of options; He can fix it, and only He can get the credit. It's those testimonies that we are able to share with others to encourage them to believe and know that our Heavenly Father can do big things not just in the Bible or in our life, but in the lives of those around us also.

Now, I say all this, but also with a caveat. Having spent many years around the Church, I have to admit, I have seen all kinds of silly stuff. Unfortunately, people's actions do not always represent God well, and sometimes bring confusion or even disconnection. So, if you are thinking, man, the supernatural stuff I have seen from some Christians is not connecting me to God, or bringing about the goodness of God, I can understand. But just because someone does a bad job of representing how to bake a cake does not mean cakes are all bad. It is the same with the supernatural. We really have to judge people by their fruit and the quality of their relationships, not what they say or do.

I'll never forget when I had only been saved for a couple years and was going to a charismatic church. They were great people, and I had a great pastor. I still love them to this day. But one day, there was an instance that lacked a lot of maturity and understanding. There was a young girl in her teens who came in, and if I remember right, was a little disruptive during the service. After the service, there was an altar call and she came up to get prayer. During prayer she started to manifest demons, and I saw things I had never seen before.

She had physical strength that was unnatural for a girl that size, she started hissing like a snake, and her head was twisting around in a way that was completely unexplainable. Several elders started to pray over her, and the more they prayed the more the demons would manifest—this went on for over an hour. At one point, an elder took a Bible and started hitting her over the head with the Bible and screaming, "In Jesus' name come out". As I recall this memory, I can't help but laugh at this and yet feel heartache for that young lady. She needed help and deliverance from the demons that were terrorizing her, but she didn't need a Bible over her head. The focus in that situation was on the physical Bible and not the source. The power comes from the source who spoke it.

I believe when it comes to the supernatural, it can become much like this situation. We can focus more on the acts of what's going on and not where it's coming from. We get so caught up in the moment because it's amazing and breathtaking that we lose focus on the one whom it came from. The supernatural should be an overflow of who we are and a byproduct of our relationship with God. When we focus on Him and what He's doing, then the supernatural will flow around us, and it shouldn't surprise us. If we focus on what He can do for us, it will dry up. We will lose out on a beautiful relationship and the benefits of having it.

Here is another story that I think brings home the point that God's love can transform us and reach us in powerful ways when we see his supernatural work. For many years, Kasey and I desired to build our dream home—Kasey mor so than me, because it's been a desire of her heart since she was a little girl to have a stable home. From the time Kasey was in elementary school until she graduated high school, she had moved somewhere between twenty-five and thirty times. That's hard to even wrap my mind around. As you can imagine, any person would want some stability after that.

We had tried to sell our house several times, and things just didn't seem to work out. We couldn't even get our house to show much at the time, and if we did, the offers just weren't very good. We finally decided we would give it one last try and see what happened. We thought we had at least six to eight months before our house would sell, and we were way wrong. It sold within a month!

This posed another problem, because there were no rental properties within sixty miles that would fit our family. On top of all that, we still had to work out the financing to build our house. There were so many things at the time that it made it seem impossible for us to build. I can't remember the exact number, but on at least four or five occasions, I told Kasey we could build and then something would fall through on either the land, the financing, or both. At one point, Kasey said she didn't believe it was going to happen.

In the natural world, I didn't believe it either, but something supernatural rose up in me and I knew it would. Kasey has always been the one in our family to believe in crazy, and this time she just didn't have the faith. That's what God gives us each other for. It was my turn this time to believe in something that seemed impossible. God wanted to fulfill a desire and dream that Had been in Kasey's heart (His daughter's heart), for years. God was going to allow me to partner with Him not to just believe, but to actually build it and see it through.

Long story short, after months of ups and downs and everything in between, it came to pass, but the ending was the icing on the cake and it couldn't have been better. When I called the bank to ask them when we could close, they set a date and I couldn't believe my ears. I even repeated the date to the lady and asked her if that's what she said. She said yes, that's correct, will that work? Heck yeah that will work! That day was Kasey's birthday! I couldn't think of a better day.

Only God, Kasey's Heavenly Father, could have made that happen. It was so divine and supernatural it was hilarious. It was like Him saying I love you and I told you so at the same time. It's things like this that blow my mind, and He continues to show me His love toward me and those around me. I knew He wanted to show up in a big way for us—I took those words He spoke, believed them, and spoke them out loud until I saw the impossible become possible.

As mentioned before, obedience brings power for transformation. But the biggest reason that happens is because obedience allows us to stay connected to God in the natural realm, as well as in the spiritual realm. The separation between God's normal or natural and our normal or natural is sin. We have allowed sin and disobedience in our lives, and it keeps us from seeing God work in ways he always intended. The crux of what he intended was to always be in relationship with us. Not a relationship that is just in our mind, but also in our spirit. This place of connection with God is what allows us to fully hear and know the words God has for us and for us to share with others.

If we are not open to supernatural connection with God, we will, in many ways, limit the power of our words. If we are not open to supernatural connection with God, we will not hear or believe the words He wants us to speak out for transformation. We will miss them! It's like we're a superhero with superpowers that do not always make sense to the natural or logical world. But when we're trying to help save the day, it's like saying we won't use those powers and just want to try to help without those powers that some might not understand or believe in. It is ridiculous to think that. And yet, many of us, because of pride or other issues, are trying to do just that—we're trying to use our natural minds or natural thoughts to speak God's words, instead of being open to speak things from Him, even when they do not always make sense.

Transforming Steps:

1. Think of a time that you experienced something supernatural or unexplainable from God. How did this

bring you closer to Him and how did it transform you (even in a small way)?

2. What can you do today to bring more connection between your supernatural and natural awareness?

3. What supernatural power can you engage with in your natural world today? Belief? Faith? Prayer? Healing? Faith?

Chapter Eight

TRANSFORMING THE WORLD

"Now is the time I really want you to start to think about how God's word can make not only your life come alive and transform, but how God might want to use you to transform the world! When you start speaking God's words over your life, you will realize even more that there are not only supernatural powers at work, but there are also invisible powers at work.

Words Have Power: It's a Law!

The invisible power of our words is not supernatural. It is different, because the fact that our words are powerful is actually a law. We must think of words like we think of gravity, or oxygen. Both are invisible; both are necessary to live on this Earth. These powers exist to everyone living in the world, even if we do not want to acknowledge it or think about it. If I throw something up in the air, or drop something off a building, it's only a matter of time until it is coming down. Gravity is a law created by God that affects us every day. If we take a breath, we get oxygen; now, we do not see the oxygen, and we do not see the air outside, but we do see the impact of the air on a windy day, when it blows branches out of trees, and we do see the impact of oxygen in the air if we try to breathe underwater.

Just like gravity, there is a law that God put in place that says our words are powerful. The words we speak are much like gravity around us. They affect and impact us every day — even if we do not see the power, we see the impact of the power. Hebrews 4:12 says, "For the word of God is alive and active. Sharper than any double-edged sword, it penetrates even to dividing soul and spirit, joints and marrow." (Hebrews 4:12) Jeremiah 1:12 says, "Then the LORD said to me, 'You have seen well, for I am watching over my word to perform it.'" When the words you speak come from God and His heart, he will watch over them in the invisible realm to make sure His word comes to pass.

When I started to become aware of the law about our words, the impact was tremendous. I hope as you have been reading this book, you have started to see that, too. By speaking His words over my business, I started seeing business and people come into my life like I had never seen. I was no longer striving for work but now aligning myself with His will for me. If I'm seated with Christ and a co-heir, then I need to realize it. I'm blessed and anointed, and by speaking and acting like I am, it changed my life. It even made me start realizing how much more loved I am than I thought. God's word impacts every area of our lives; we just have to take the time to listen, so we can release and walk in it.

When your words come from God, they have so much power. They can impact your life, or even change a nation. The Bible has so many stories of this, but one of my favorites is in Nehemiah. Nehemiah was not some hot-shot celebrity, or some big man with big power. He was a slave in another country working for a king as the cup bearer. Talk about a lack of big significance from the world's eyes! I wonder if he wished he could have more impact in the world, or if he realized that actually, being a cupbearer to the king, day after boring day , meant he was perfectly positioned for what God had for him to do. In this story, word had come back to him about the Holy Land, His home, that the city walls had been torn down and the gates were in ruins. It says he grieved for days, praying and fasting over this.

In Chapter One, it says he repented on behalf of himself and the nation as well. He also refers to the God of unfailing love and asks Him to grant Him success with the king and that the king would favor him. This is very wise on Nehemiah's part, because he realizes that without this favor, not only will he not be able to leave, but he won't have the resources to rebuild it. After Nehemiah prays this, he chooses his words very wisely when the king asks him what is wrong. After he tells him of his distress and sadness over what happened, the king asks him what he can do to help. Nehemiah is prepared with an answer, and expresses the word of God, executing wisely.

In Chapter Two, you will see that he asks for lumber and safe passage through these areas that he would travel. He tells the king he needs letters addressed to certain people that are in charge of these areas. He prays, and receives God's word for the situation, then follows through with action as well. Nehemiah uses his words wisely when speaking and comes prepared. Before he did all this, let's remember what he did at the beginning. It says he prayed and fasted over the situation. I believe He went to God, received God's heart for the situation, received His favor, and was able to carry out what seemed like an impossible task. It's a remarkable story about leadership, courage and wisdom. I highly recommend you finish the story and see what he is able to accomplish.

Keep Growing and Practicing!

But just because we know the power of words, and have the right heart behind them, doesn't mean we always get it right. That is okay. As long as we are growing and learning.

I'm sure many of you have made decisions to do things without proper respect for gravity at some point, and you've fallen over. I know I have! In the same way, we can do things without proper respect for the power of our words, and fall over emotionally or spiritually, but we can always get back up again!

This happened to me recently, so I am not immune! Not too long ago, I had several difficult customers all at once. Instead of speaking life over my life and business, I started saying things like, "I hate our line of work," "I always get rude and difficult people," and on and on and on. It's one thing to have a bad thought; it's another thing to provide the thought a playground in your head to play! For a couple weeks, I built a theme park in my head and invited all the bad thoughts to come and stay without kicking them out.

Once I came to my senses, I realized I was only damaging myself and my life and motivation toward my work. I repented by changing my ways; I asked God to forgive me. I prayed out loud and said, "I rebuke and cancel all the negative words I spoke, and I release God's favor over my business." I started to speak blessings over people I was working for and dealing with. People's attitudes changed and the environment changed. I can't repeat enough how important the words we speak are. They are life and they are death! When we decide to speak the words of God who created all life, then things start to grow. God's words have allowed me to speak life into dead areas in my life and see growth where there was no hope.

My point in saying all this is that beating ourselves up does not change the words we spoke. But new words do! When you start to use your words to see transformation, do not get discouraged. You will slip up—we all will. But thank God, He will cover us with His love.

Let Your Old Man Die

Another key point I have mentioned before (but is worth mentioning again) is to remember that as you transform your world with your words, you have to be willing to let your old self die. I recently watched an old favorite movie of mine called The Count of Monte Cristo. I'm sorry if I spoil it for you, but to make a long story short, an innocent man named Edmond spends thirteen years in prison, and during that time receives training from another cellmate in weapons and economics. Edmond becomes friends with this man, who leaves him a map that leads to unprecedented fortune. This map does not leave an exact location but a series of clues and riddles he must piece together to find it. When Edmond discovers it, he and his friend realize it is more than they could have ever been imagined. He also realizes he can no longer use his current name, and so changes his name to The Count of Monte Cristo. He refers to his old self as dead. He goes on to tell several other people that Edmond is dead. There's a lot of imagery here that we can take away from this.

God's word is much like this treasure that Edmond found, but far more valuable. In the movie and in life, treasure is great, but it only has so much worth and lasting value, unlike God's Word which is priceless and lasts forever. When we find the treasure of God's word and spend it by applying it to our lives, there are things that take place that are supernatural. Isaiah 55:11 tells us that His word does not return void. The New Living Translation puts it this way — "It is the same with my word. I send it out, and it always produces fruit. It will accomplish all I want it to, and it will prosper everywhere I send it."

The treasure that we must discover is not just simple words written in a book, but the exact words the Father is speaking over us and our current situation. We need to set our eyes on the Father and say what He is saying. When we do this, we are being the ambassadors that Paul spoke about. We are decreeing God's word over our lives, workplace, family, and everything else we do. God doesn't just want to impact a small piece of our world, He wants to impact all of it. His word transforms situations, our situations.

This being alive and dead to your past self and words is not just something you do in church or around spiritual people. And even if you have been going to church your whole life, you might have to die to the self that thought they had things figured out, or the self that harshly criticizes your neighbors or family. Many of us have spent years compartmentalizing our lives and cutting off potential fruit when we do that. Take for example the guy who told me "Church is church and business is business." I'm still laughing at that one. Everything we allow ourselves to think and believe carries over into all areas of our lives. People must realize that God's word is meant to impact every area of our lives.

Bad water or lack of sun will damage the potential of a fruit that comes from a tree or prevent it from bearing fruit at all. It will still have the potential, but it will never realize the full potential and be fully fulfilled without the things it needs. Well, God's Word is life to us—it contains all we need to reach our full potential. On the other hand, bad words can damage the size and potential of our impact and joy in this world. There are consequences if you do not respect the power of your words.

Bringing God's Restoration Through Words
Since the fall of man, God's plan has always been about restoration—showing us His love, and bringing things back into order. Satan's plan, on the other hand, has been to destroy what God has created, including us and everything around us. God said he gave us dominion over the Earth and everything in it. I love Genesis, because it shows us how things

were supposed to be when God created them. Everything was good! It talks about the Earth being formless and the Spirit of God hovering over the earth. God spoke and things started to take form. The supernatural God invaded the natural with His words, and things were transformed. It also says that you and I were made in His likeness. In proverbs it says that life and death are in the power of the tongue, and those who love it will eat its fruit (Proverbs 18:21). I look at these Scriptures as a puzzle piece that has existed for thousands of years that we get the pleasure of putting together to empower our lives today.

What I love about the Father is it's not like He's saying, "You messed it up really bad, now figure it out and go fix it." Not even close! He wants to co-create with us. He is coming alongside us and giving us the answers when we decide to ask, along with the tools to get there. God's plan has always been for His children to rule and reign from the top of the seven mountains. To bring love, truth, and justice from these places. It is so important we operate from these places. There is a lost and dying world out there that needs His love and restoration.

So what is your next step? To make an impact in the kingdom, you, like Nehamiah, need to recognize your area of influence. I recently had to sit back and reevaluate my situation. I found myself wishing for a bigger platform or even envying people who are getting to speak and teach from bigger stages. I'm just being very real and honest here, so please don't judge me. What I had to do is sit back and look at my "Kingdom," my area of influence. The people I have the most impact on are my wife, my kids, and people at work. I have done a decent job, but I know I could do better. We all have a kingdom of people around us. Who are the people you can influence that are already around you?

I look at Joseph's life, and the Word says that God blessed Joseph's hands in all he did. Potopher didn't even have to worry about anything except what He would eat and drink in his house. I want to be like that. I could have all the impact in the world, but If I don't take care of my biggest blessings first, I have lost vision of what's most important. Do your very best with what you have and more will be given. There's nothing wrong with thinking big and shooting for the stars, just make sure you take care of what you have first, do the best you can, and be thankful for what you have.

Just like Nehemiah, every one of us is called to something and created for a purpose. That means YOU are called to something and created for a purpose. Each purpose is unique! I have spent the last three years interviewing people all over the world on my podcast *Are You Real* discussing this very subject. If you're not familiar with it, then you can get on iTunes or Google Play and download it now. Like right now! Stop reading this and pick up your phone—I'm telling you to get sidetracked and go download it, because there are so many people I have had the privilege to interview that have transformed my life! I know their thoughts and words will transform your life as you hear them.

Okay, back on track now, we all have a purpose and ability to impact an area where we are called. Just like Adam in Genesis, we have an area of influence that no one else has that we are called to. We were designed uniquely with our gifts, talents, personality, and life circumstances to impact it. We must discover and take authority to the areas God has called us to and take action. If we will take the time to listen to what He is saying and doing, we can have an impact this world has never seen.

My friend Robby Dawkins has a story about how this plays out. He was driving one day and saw a woman with her hazard lights on. He felt the leading of God and pulled over to the side of the road and asked if he could help. The woman had run out of gas, and so he offered to get her some gas. He went home and got a lawnmower tank with gas and gave it to her. She reached to give him money from her purse, but Robby just told her that he wanted her to know that Jesus loved her and he didn't want any money. He said God had put it in their heart to stop, not their own thoughts or minds.

I will finish the story in a moment, but first I want to say that I love this story, because it ties together a lot of what we're talking about. Robby heard from God, was obedient, then spoke life with both words and actions. So what happened next?

The woman started to tear up and asked if he really believed what he said. Robby said he did and ended up leading her to Christ. Ten years later, she started working for Robby's doctor's office. She had been going to church and growing in her faith ever since that encounter. When he came into the doctor's office, she would introduce him to others in the waiting room and ask him to tell them what he told her on the side of the road that day. He ended up leading about five more people to God in the waiting room because of the impact of one act of supernatural kindness, and words of love that were encased in a somewhat-natural process. Not only that, but the doctor himself was so impacted by Robby's kindness to the receptionist that he stopped charging him, and Robby didn't have to pay a medical bill for years! This story reminds me that even acts of kindness and communicating God's kindness have supernatural powers attached to them and can transform people in a miraculous way! The transformation we sow and give away to others can also create opportunities for our own transformation in our personal life! We transform together as we hear and live out the word of God.

Overcoming Opposition With Relationship

As we get God's heart and start to speak His words into opportunities, we may find ourselves in a lot of opposition. We are constantly at war with Satan and his minions. The Word says we don't wrestle against flesh and blood, but principalities and invisible powers (Ephesians 6:12). Powers like the desire to speak badly about a situation, when we know we can speak good. The enemy's goal is to destroy everything God has made.

The good news is that Romans 8:31 says, "What, then, shall we say in response to these things? If God is for us, who can be against us?" And Romans 8:37 says, "In all these things we are more than conquerors through him who loved us." We are victorious and we need to make sure we understand that. We don't fight to be victorious, we fight because we are victorious. Jesus has already won the battle; we just need to make sure we are fighting the right battles and He's in them.

How we feel about things and what is actually happening I believe are usually not the same, especially when we are in a fight. I spent most of my early adult life speaking negatively over our businesses and finances. I would say things like, "We are broke, we can't do this, we're going to lose everything," and on and on I'd go. It was terrible, and thank you Jesus I have a spirit-filled wife who won't listen to my stupidity and will call me out on it and help correct me. She was nice about it, but she flat-out told me to stop because we were getting the fruits of my lips and I was killing us. I was allowing the fiery darts of the enemy to come out of my mouth.

I have found in my life that the way I think things should look and what God is doing are usually different. Heck, it's even Scriptural. The word says that his ways are not our ways and His thoughts are not our thoughts. The truth is that he sees the big picture. The hardest part about that is when we don't realize this, we can start to doubt ourselves, Him, and the situation around us. It's so important for us to pray and get the Father's Heart on a situation so we can be in step with Him. When we do this, there's encouragement in our spirit that helps us push through to see what He is doing. It's then we start to see doors open up and see God's favor on us to see things through. The test is to see if there's God's favor in the situation and doors are being opened up. That's how we can tell if we are in the right spot at the right time.

The easiest way to get aligned with God and His transformative words that unlock the potential in your life is simply to spend time with Him, to get to know God's heart and go in the direction He is headed. It is also important to have like-minded friends in your circle to encourage you on your way. We weren't created to do things on our own, and there is no lone ranger in the Kingdom of God. Ask God who needs to be in your life, and surround yourself with the right people. Find people who are willing to go on this journey of changing your words with you and help you when things get hard, or you trip up. Find people who will speak words of life over you and whom you can speak words of life over, and you will see this transformation begin to happen at a dizzying rate.

So, the way to start making a difference in the world through your words is first to recognize that whatever you choose to say, God has given us each, saved or unsaved, power in our words. Our words are powerful like gravity is powerful. We can't escape it, so to bring healthy things to people in our world, we must respect the power of our words. Secondly, we should consider our sphere of influence and life purpose. Who are the people whom God has positioned you around to help? What are the words that need to be released into their lives, or situations? Finally, we must get the words from God. We cannot be in a place of pride where we think we know better than God what is needed. Like Nehemiah, we must humbly pursue His words for a situation and then follow through with action when it is needed. How can we speak life over our purpose and calling and the people we encounter as we engage in our calling? By answering these questions, we will be well on our way to help transform the power of God to others through our words and how we speak.

Transforming Steps:

1. Who is someone in your sphere of influence whom you see every day and whom you can speak words of life to?
2. Who has spoken words of life that transformed you? Take the time to consider thanking them for what they did.
3. What would change if you believed the fact that words have power was a law like gravity?

Chapter Nine

GOD'S KINGDOM ALIVE IN YOU

"God, our Heavenly Father, has been in pursuit of us since we were born. There is an undying love and compassion toward us that is awaiting our understanding. How we show up in the world makes all the difference. There never has been and never will be anyone like you. They could clone you, have an exact lookalike, but that person would never have the same life experiences and soul as you. It's important to understand that you are one-of-a-kind and the world needs every bit of you to show up. God is looking to partner up with people who are comfortable with who they are and what He wants to do. God doesn't need you or I, but He chooses every day to reach out to us and impact others' lives.

You and I are created in His image, which means we can impact people through love and truth like nobody else. You have the ability to bring God's kingdom to Earth in a way no one else in history has. The world is struggling with an identity issue, because they don't know who they are. Satan has blinded their eyes to make them believe lies about themselves and others. We have an opportunity not to judge people for the sin that they are in, but to love them into the person God created them to be through our words and actions. We can be an extension of Jesus to a lost and confused world, but we have to show up in all of who we are.

Leading Others to Transformation

I want to give you an example of how this mandate to use our words to transform the world and others can sometimes feel overly simple, but can actually be very powerful! Several years ago, I went on a mission trip with my daughter to rebuild people's houses in Oklahoma. Our team was split up amongst hundreds of workers, and my team went and worked on a roof. Each day that we were there, there was a team leader who was asked to lead a Bible study and prayer. When my day came, I was a little nervous, because I knew theologically we had different backgrounds. (I hate to even use terms like that, because I feel like it just separates people, but it will help you get the idea.) I have been to many different churches and denominations over the years, and I can find something for me in all of them. If they are teaching Jesus and He's the focus on changing our life, then I'm all in. What I do find though is I have a preference and I tend to lean more to the non-denominational or what some would call charismatic. (I get a kick out of the word non-denominational, because it's still a denomination.)

The group I was with was younger adults, and the majority were Baptist. I knew if I started throwing around terms like "prophetic," I was going to lose a crowd and group of people REALLY fast. It's not that they weren't up for what I had to say, I just knew after spending a couple days with them that the right words were needed to teach. When it was my turn to teach, we all got into a circle at lunch in front of the house. There were about twenty people, and I remember laughing because we were in a pretty rough neighborhood and there were people walking by. The looks on their faces were funny, because you could tell they were wondering what in the world was going on.

My question to everyone in the group was, can they hear God's voice? The majority told me they couldn't, and what was interesting was that I had several pastors in our group. I went on to tell them it's much easier than they think, and asked them if they would like to do an activation.

I asked one person from the group to come sit in the middle of everyone, and we asked God what He had to say about that person. As we went around the group, you could just feel the atmosphere change. People went from being nervous to realizing they had something to say and it was relevant. People's faces lit up and they were excited. After we did that a couple times, I tried something I had seen my mentor, Bill Johnson, do from Trinity in Amarillo. We put another person in the middle, but this time everyone just got to speak one word they were hearing. I took my phone out, and as we went around I typed in that word in the order I received them.

At the very end, I took all those words and said, this is what the Lord is saying to you, and I put all the words together. I could feel the power come all over me and it was amazing. The young lady was in tears and said those were words she needed to hear and had even been praying about. After we finished up our lesson, one young lady came up to me and asked if I was using an app on my iPhone to put that strand of words together that everyone had spoken. What she didn't realize was I was allowing The Holy Spirit to speak through me and put all those words together for her. I fell over laughing. It gave me an opportunity to explain to them the power of stepping into hearing God's voice for our lives and stepping into what we are called to do. What we all just experienced was Heaven's words invading earth and breaking into the atmosphere to change people's lives. It was powerful and life-changing. Not only did God's words get spoken, people's blind eyes were open to the truth—THEY

COULD HEAR! Sometimes, it is much easier than we think. After reading about God in the Bible, even if you do not hear a word directly from Him, you can repeat a verse or an idea that is Biblically sound and lined up with His written word, but just the act of speaking it out over someone who may need to hear God's thoughts for them in that moment is incredibly powerful!

Implementing Words of Life Together

If you are struggling with something, or know someone who is, I want you to encourage them by speaking words of life and connection to them. It saddens me that for so many years I saw people in church act like everything was okay. I believe they thought they had to because there wasn't an environment cultivated to talk about their struggles. The truth is we all have struggles and fears. I know when Ester had to go before the King to save her people, she wasn't like, "Here I am, now listen to me!" She knew the King could have her killed for showing up uninvited. Heck, she was the Queen and still couldn't do that. It's okay to have fears and struggle with sin issues no matter how big or small. It's not ok to hide them and tuck them away. The truth is, until we bring them to the light, expose them for the nasty little lies they are, they just keep getting bigger until we feel overwhelmed by them.

Every temptation starts out small—the devil doesn't show up in a red suit with a pitchfork trying to talk us into something we don't want to do. It always looks tempting and innocent until we step into his traps; that's why we need each other for accountability and someone to lean on. When we are open about our struggles and fears, it not only brings them to the light but gives permission to other people to be honest. It creates an environment for things to be exposed for what they are and allows God's words and love and truth to break through and penetrate the lies. If you are struggling to believe the words of God over you or another person or situation, it is okay and healthy to be honest about it. There is no condemnation in Christ Jesus, and through this book, I have tried to model that I am not perfect, and I don't always get it right, but I can keep trying and be grateful for the moment I do get it!

The world, when living under Satan's authority, has been blind to how good our Heavenly Father is and how much He loves us. Authority was given to man in the garden to rule and reign on this earth. When Adam disobeyed, he handed his rightful authority and rule over to Satan. Jesus died for more than just our sin and disobedience. It's deeper than that—He died so that we could come back into our rightful place of ruling and reigning.

To be imitators of Christ and to walk in the fullness of our destiny, we must speak life to those around us and speak identity into them. We all have a territory or a domain that God called us to be an ambassador to. It can be at school, family, work, or anywhere else we spend our time. We get to choose to show up in all of God's Glory and affect the atmosphere around us. As we do, we can lift people up or bring them down with us. Life and death are in the power of our tongue, and God created you and me to have life and to have an abundance of it. It is our job to show up where we are and bring Heaven to Earth and change the atmosphere around us.

What Does the Kingdom Look Like?
The Kingdom is God's original plan and design for something. Let's take what I do by trade for an example. I build, remodel and flip homes. During the years I can't tell you how many times I have seen contractors show up, do a terrible job and leave people hanging with a half-completed job while taking all their money. One story that hit me the hardest was when my friend and I were called up to finish

a job in a small town. When we got there, her bathroom was about 90 percent done, and she had a patio that was being built that was about 10 percent started, and all the concrete needed to be taken out because the finish was so bad.

The worst part about that was the guy was paid in full. He gave this lady a long sob story about how he had hit hard times. She was a very kind, giving and trusting person and wanted to help him. Well, he never showed back up. We had to take over the job, and to be honest, I didn't want it, but I wanted to help her. We finished the bathroom first and started tearing out the patio, and the project ended up being beautiful. Almost every day, we prayed with that woman because she was in tears over her hard-earned money being taken from her. She lost about $30,000-$40,000. I tell you this story because that was not and never will be God's plan or design for the construction industry or any other. His kingdom and plan for where we work is truth, honesty, integrity, and love.

Jesus summed up all the law (and I believe our kingdom mandate) when He said, "Love your neighbor as yourself." If we are in a healthy place in our lives, we will never want to be lied to, stolen from, or hurt. God's kingdom looks like the fruits of the spirit in that situation and place. If you're not sure if God's kingdom is showing up around you, then ask yourself if you see His fruits there. If not, then it's our job to take them there and change the atmosphere and situation. It's a great opportunity to go to the Father in our prayer time and ask Him what he wants to do. The beautiful thing is we don't have to figure it out—He already has a perfect plan, we just need to listen and partner up with Him to do it. Like Ester in the Bible, we were created for such a time as this, right now! You and I have an opportunity to bring God's redemption, power and love to any industry. God wants to bring change everywhere, and it starts with us willing to listen and obey.

God has always had an amazing plan for Earth and created us to partner with Him to create amazing things to manage here. One of the biggest hurdles I had to get over in my life and I see in so many others is the fact we are abundantly loved. For so many years I looked at myself as worthless and sinful. That was far from the truth, and that's what Satan wanted me to believe. Since I confessed my sins and gave my life in surrender to Christ and what He did, I have been a new man. We all still stumble and fall, but we are always loved and He is always there waiting to pick us up and move forward.

When we discover His love and realize we have authority again, it's a game changer in our lives. We start to operate from a place of royalty instead of as slaves. We are now able to listen to what the Father is doing, what He always wanted to do on Earth, and start speaking those things over our lives. Gods words don't return void, but ours do. It's so important that we, like Jesus, see what the Father is doing and do those things, hear what He is doing, listen, and speak them like Ezekiel did. There are dry bones all around us that only God can make alive. God never intended for them to die, but he is waiting for you and me to speak life and resurrection power over them to come to life. This is your mandate to the world.

Transforming Steps:

1. In the beginning, I asked you who you might take with you on this journey. Now, I am wondering how can you expand your support and create a group or band of brothers and sisters whom you can speak life over and who can speak life over you?
2. How can you bring the Kingdom of God into your awareness and life today?

3. Who is in your life right now whom you can help and support by speaking God's words of love and transformation over them?

Chapter Ten: Bonus Chapter

HEARING GOD'S TRANSFORMATION PLAN

"I know what you're thinking, it seems like the book ended, why is it still going? Well, the truth is that as I began asking around to find out more about how people hear from God, I was so inspired and empowered by what I learned that I didn't want to hold back any good thing from you! I couldn't live with myself knowing I could learn so many life-changing things and not pass them on.

I want to leave you with a way to continue to explore your own journey of hearing God, that (quite frankly) has less to do with me, and more to do with God and the multitude of voices and wisdom of people that have been following God and hearing His voice well. I can think of no better way to close this book than to share the inspiration and empowerment that I have received from the mighty men and women who graciously contributed their time, thoughts and gifts to help all of us get to know God and His voice, more intimately! I hope you are encouraged and excited, and that your heart is awakened to hear the love the Father has for you.

God's Voice Brings Freedom and Love
Brad McClendon

Everything and every way that God speaks to us can be easily identified as being from God, because it puts your mind toward Jesus, not yourself, and not someone else. Anything that speaks to you that doesn't magnify Jesus is from a different spirit. We are told in 1st John to test every spirit. Why? Because everything from God points to God and to Jesus.

How do I hear God? I would say that I'm a seer by gifting; I became spirit-filled at age five and I had some amazing encounters with God. I would see things in the spirit. For years, whatever I would see, I would do. Jesus said, in John 5:19, that He only did what He saw the Father doing. But He also only says what He hears the father saying. So there are different ways to be able to hear the Lord. Initially, in my life, I was hearing the Lord by seeing visions.

One example of this happened one day when I was sitting in my La-Z-Boy Chair. My relationship with God was not in the best place at that time. But suddenly, I got a vision and I saw myself going to Bi-Lo. In the vision, I found someone walking down the aisle and saw myself say something to her. When I get a vision, I always check to see where it comes from. I know, for me, I didn't care about going to Bi-Lo. But for me, in that vision, I was enamored that Jesus was magnified in my mind. And that's the way you know it is not you: everything you see and hear points to Jesus. So, I knew it was Jesus, because the vision was secondary to the presence that I felt from the Lord.

So, I had the vision, and then checked for confirmation of Jesus, and then I got up and went to Bi-Lo in obedience. I walked down the aisle, and remember, I am used to seeing visions, but this time, I heard something in my mind. I heard "Reese's," like the candy. It made no sense, to my mind or logic. But that is what Romans says when it talks about the carnal mind being at enmity with God.

When I heard "Reese's," I knew it was Jesus. Why? Because that same presence of God rose up in me. But, how do you start that conversation with a stranger in an aisle? Before I could talk myself out of it, I turned to the girl and say, "Hey, Reese's."

When I said that, the girl fell on the floor. Everyone else left the aisle, because the girl started crying. I went to help her up and I ask her what Reese's means to her.

She said, "I know this is God."

I said, "Why do you say this God?"

And she said, "Because my dad died. And he used to call me his little Reese's."

She knew that that was Jesus, because the same presence came upon the Word. And that's the main thing that I look for even when people are talking, I'm always looking for that presence, that truth, any type of truth that sets us free. It magnifies the Lord, because only the Lord can set us free. So real truth or the real voice of God not only tells you what to do, but there should be some freedom in it, because there's truth in it, because it's actually carrying the person of Jesus.

I couldn't wait to go home and talk to the Lord. That is another truth I have realized. If you hear for others, you still go away wanting to be closer to the Lord, not closer to that person. I asked Him why he did that, why He gave me that word and spoke to me. I felt He told me He did it to get me back on track. I had been in a rut for some time, but He is the path of life (John 14:6). He said He sent His kindness that caused me to repent back to Him (Romans 2:4). And that's also what happened to that girl. He caused her to repent, but not by preaching to her to tell her problems and what she was doing wrong. He actually gave her kindness by speaking a prophetic word that led her back to Jesus and, of course, caused her to remember love. The love that she had from her father. If there's anything the voice of God does, it's bring people out of the pit and back to love.

What about what happens when it is not from God? I think some people are gifted in hearing prophetically, and they rely on their own gift, without God. If we are naturally gifted in hearing spiritual things, there are a lot of temptations where the enemy can get us. Maybe we have a need and we turn on our gift to make everything happen. Then after it's over, we say it's the Lord, but the results of that the nature of that is that we are worn out. There's no life in it. There's no Jesus. And Jesus came to give life. So when you start hearing those voices that get you in the flesh to use your gifting, you'll find out that the fruit of that voice, after it's all over, it has worn you out. And the voice that speaks from truly above is the voice that actually magnifies Jesus and engrafts life in your system, and graphs life in your heart, and then what you do is out of rest instead of out of fear. And at the end, if you have heard the Lord, you have rest, you have life, and you look at everything that you've done, and you realize, man, I didn't do this. The Lord did it. I partnered with Him. And so everything now that you do has an anointing of Jesus on it, which magnifies the Lord.

Even though I have shared about hearing God for other people, I want to make it clear that the voice of God is first for us. If we listen, we start getting addicted to listening to His voice, and it will transform us first. That way, we can transform others. You really can't transform other people without you first being transformed. That is something I've learned from Bob Jones, my spiritual father. I'd come to him and hear these things from God. And I would tell him what the Lord said to me, and I would be so excited and want to share with everyone, but he would say; "You might want to listen to your message first." That is because the voice of God is for us to be turned and transformed and to put us on the path of life. So, regardless of what we hear and who we hear from, or who we hear for, if it is from God, it will bring us closer to God, and it will transform us to want more of God.

For more information on Brad McClendon, check out https://livingvineministries.org.

The Holy Spirit, The Great Counselor
Danny Silk

Love transforms us, and the power of love is the power to defeat fear. The ongoing conversation that I have with folks is that love and fear are in a mortal battle. And the power of love is what gives me the equipment over the power of fear. The power of love allows me to realize that I'm connected to the Holy Spirit, instead of the spirit of fear. Whenever I get hurt, I scared or threatened, I have the equipment I need to get out.

I think most of us lose sight of who our counselor is. And so we choose the wrong counselor. The power of love is in choosing of the Holy Spirit to be my counselor through the disconnects, through the uncertainty, through hurt, fear, whatever it might be. When I don't have the power of love, fear occupies that same spot. In 1 John 4:18, it says that perfect love casts out fear. But it is also true that fear casts out love. And so we have to make that choice.

A little while back, Sherry and I were pretty disconnected. I don't remember why, I just remember that it was a serious, serious disconnect. And we hadn't had one in quite some time. And she was shutting down, she was going to a bad place. I could see it. And I was scared. I wanted to go to a bad place myself. And it was right there. Where I said, "My goal with you is connection. I love you. I don't know what we're going to do right now. But my goal with you is connection."

And as soon as I said those words, I remember just feeling the fear drain right out of me. I relaxed and the best Danny showed up. It really helped us, because I didn't jump into the same hole she was in. I think love and hope are the characteristics of being children of God. And both of those things help us to eradicate the stronghold that shame would like to have. So love and hope are the things that give me power over shame.

Shame is really an identity tag. It tries to associate my who with my what. But even if I did something, it doesn't actually change my who. Shame says you didn't make a mistake, you are a mistake. You know, you didn't fail, you are a failure, you didn't just do something bad, you are bad. And so love and hope are the keys that allow me to stay rooted in love. I am deeply loved, and I have hope to grow and to change through this mistake.

In a big way, giving power to love is how I invite the kingdom of God into the world around me. I bring the kingdom to the world by agreeing with my Dad. My Father has a certain way of doing things. I'm learning more and more and more every day what those things are and how He does them. But what I do know when I make an agreement with and act consistent with that, is that then His kingdom comes through my life. I get to put my Daddy on display. I think that's really what I'm here to do, is to show people who my Father is and who He is to them. The Kingdom of Heaven is righteousness, peace and joy. It's pretty simple. It's not very convoluted or complex. It's knowing who I am and not giving into shame. It's authority over chaos where I can bring love and peace.

To find out more about Danny Silk, you can visit https://www.lovingonpurpose.com.

Signs from God
Seth Dahl

Hearing God has been the single most important factor in both my life as well as my family's. I invested ten years on staff at Bethel Church in Redding, CA. As I was coming up on my ninth year, I began to feel like something was going to change. I became unsettled, but not in an unhealthy way, in a way where my wife and I could sense God was the one causing it. After a few conversations with leaders and many late nights processing with my wife about it all, one night in particular she looked over at me as I read a line in a book: "Coincidence is a language of the Spirit". As I read the sentence, she announced, "If you don't leave soon, you are going to overstay your time here."

I heard what she said but was preoccupied, because as she said it, a ladybug walked across the ceiling above her. It was not the season for ladybugs, so I watched it closely while my wife thought I wasn't paying attention. She looked at me again and told me I should listen to her, to which I replied that I'd heard her loud and clear, pointing at the ceiling. I'd once heard that ladybugs can be a sign of God's Anointing. To me, the ladybug was a confirmation from God about what my wife had just said.

Several years earlier, I was interviewing people for a job opening in our ministry. We wanted to begin creating resources, so I really needed the right person. While on the phone with one of the applicants I saw a ladybug walking across a paper snowflake a child had cut out. Snowflakes are also significant for me from Isaiah 55:10, which says the Word

146

that comes down from Heaven, waters the Earth, and does not return void comes to us like snow.

Once I saw the ladybug on the snowflake, the interview process was over. I turned down two other prospects who were more qualified, because the Lord had just told me that His anointing was on His word during that interview. I hired her immediately and it was the best hiring decision I'd made at that point. She helped us create all of our resources for pastors and parents, as well as get our website up and running. The ladybug and snowflake were all I needed.

It may seem strange that I "hear" God speaking through ladybugs and paper snowflakes, but God says in Psalm 78:3-5 (ESV), "I will open my mouth in a parable; I will utter dark sayings from of old, things that we have heard and known, that our fathers have told us. We will not hide them from their children, but tell to the coming generation the glorious deeds of the LORD, and his might, and the wonders that he has done."

To me, these unusual coincidences, or "dark sayings," are one of the ways God speaks to me most. Usually, they come suddenly and "out of nowhere," but I live my life with the awareness that He could speak at any time, so I am ready for these types of interruptions.

The morning after the ladybug walked across the ceiling, I began the process of leaving the job and ministry I'd led for all those years, and that began the most intense two months we'd had as a family.

Right away ,my wife began to sense that we would leave Redding and move to Los Angeles. This sounded crazy coming from her, because her dream is to own five-hundred-plus acres and have lots of horses. I must admit, hearing her speak about moving to LA, my heart wasn't even slightly open to the idea. That is, until God spoke again.

She went out one summer night just before her birthday, and wanted to ask God for a sign of whether we were to move or not. As confirmation, she wanted lightning, thunder and rain on her birthday. Before she asked Him, she checked the weather, and rain was nowhere in sight. It was supposed to be in the 100+ temperature range with perfectly clear skies. In case you aren't familiar with Redding summers, it DOES NOT rain for nine months of the year. Knowing that, and after checking the weather, Lauren decided not to pray for the sign. She just figured if it didn't happen, she was still right about moving.

Well, the next day was her birthday, and we were outside playing with our two new puppies and some friends, when all-of-a-sudden there was a rumble in the distance. Next came the lightning, then it proceeded to pour rain as if it forgot it was still summer. We all splashed around in it since it was such a relief from the heat, when my wife looked at me and said, "Um, I need to tell you something." Needless to say my heart flung wide open to the idea of moving, so again we began the process in the days following. As the time approached for us to move, our realtor couldn't find anything that would work for us. At the time, we had two horses and three large dogs, and we wanted to keep them with us. After weeks of searching, she started typing an email to us (which she told us about later). She wrote something like "I don't think the house you want, in the area you want, with the land you want, at the price you want, is even possible".

Before she sent it, "something" told her to delete the email right away. As that was happening, Lauren came to me frustrated and sad that we hadn't found anything yet, and our plan was to move in three weeks. We took about five seconds and asked God to speak to us about what to do. Immediately, she stepped back and said she had a vision of Craigslist, then went off to grab her computer. Within minutes, she found a house in our price range, with the same square footage of the house we just sold, on the same size land (two-and-a-half acres), with a fifteen-stall horse barn and room for the dogs. She sent it to our realtor, who'd just deleted her email to us, and she wrote back right away. She said she knew the neighborhood and the house and there was no way it could be the price it was. "This house should be at least double the price," she wrote. "It has to be a scam, but I'll check on it in the morning".

The next morning, she found out it wasn't a scam, and three weeks later we moved in. Now, not only do we have our horses and dogs with us, we have two cows as well. Yes, you read that correctly. We have two cows in Los Angeles. We didn't think land like where we live even existed, but it does. We just needed to hear His voice on how to find it.

All along this adventure, we simply said yes each time He spoke. Whenever we said yes, it became easier to recognize Him speaking, and every time we obeyed, it became more normal for us to take risks that are out of this world. In all our yes's, we were also very intentional to include our children. Our choices were going to affect them greatly, and we wanted them to see not only some of the ways He speaks, but also have their part in our response to His leading.

In our lives and family, hearing His voice has been interesting, and sometimes a bit strange, but also the most exhilarating thing ever. We wouldn't want to live any other way than listening and saying yes to His words for our lives.

For more information on Seth Dahl, you can visit https://sethdahl.com.

The Most Important Voice in the World
Ambassador Dr. Clyde Rivers

I have walked with God for over thirty-one years in ministry and life. It has been an amazing journey. My life was transformed one day after hearing the voice of God myself for the first time. I knew it was God, because after I asked Jesus into my heart I had conviction over things I was doing that were wrong. I can't explain exactly what that feeling was at that time, but now I have come to understand that it was the convicting power of God.

Hearing God's voice has taken me on one of the most amazing life journeys I could have ever imagined. As a ministry leader for over twenty-five years, leading a ministry in the kingdom of God and Hearing his voice has become the guidepost for my entire life. I would hear things from God that would sound so big that my mind couldn't understand how this was going to happen. Let me give an example: one time, when God spoke to me, He told me that I was going to work with many Presidents of nations. When that thought came to my mind, my intellect said how is this going to happen, it's impossible. You don't know anyone at Presidential levels in this world. I continued to walk forward by faith. All I can tell you now is that I have worked with over fourteen presidents and First Ladies from all around the world to this day. I knew it was God's voice when he spoke to me, and I understood it because it was the same voice I heard at the time of my salvation. I didn't understand what had taken place, but I believe it to be the voice of God. Now, with all the facts and evidence, it's pretty obvious that it was the voice of God that told me I would meet and work with Presidents of other nations.

When hearing the voice of God in my life, it has been a great learning experience and an eye opener. He speaks in many different ways to me. Sometimes I just have a knowing in my mind that this is God, and it has been. I have learned to follow the leadership of the Holy Spirit in hearing the voice. The key is after you hear his voice then your actions will dictate everything. If you will act on the word from God, as if it's true, things will begin to line up with what He told you to do. You see the key to receiving the manifestation from the voice of God is the actions you take after hearing His word and the walking by faith and not by sight. After hearing the voice of God, you need to move forward believing what you heard to be truth, and that's faith. Many times, the issue that comes after hearing God's voice is waiting on the timing of God to bring the word to pass. This is a major key in moving into manifestation of the words he spoke. At this point, faith is the evidence. Your believing is the evident. God needs you at this time to hold on to the faith evidences in your mind.

Hearing the Word of the Lord through others is also vital. One day, I received a prophetic word from a top prophetic voice in the world. He told me that I was going to receive awards from the highest levels in nations for the work I had done to help humanity around the world. You know with God, all things are possible. I just received the words spoken as the Word of God. When it was spoken over me, I had no idea or any thoughts in my mind as to how this would come to pass. I just knew in my understanding, to see how this word could ever come to pass was as far out of my reach as anything in the natural realm.

Let me share with you the amazing manifestation that took place in my life. In 2017, I was a winner of a Presidential Lifetime Achievement Award, presented by the White House in the United States of America for over 4,000 volunteer service hours to make America a better place. I was truly humbled to receive this award. What I want to tell you all is that the Word that came from the man of God came to pass in my life. I received that word and it framed my life. First of all, to believe that I could receive this kind of award at a national level was really out of the range of possibility, yet little did I know it would be a Presidential award from the White House in the United States of America. When a prophetic word comes from a man or woman of God, it has to be received by the hearer as the voice of God, and you must believe it will come to pass.

It is truly possible for every person in the world to hear the voice of God. It's the most important voice you can and will ever hear, because it becomes the guiding force of your entire life. The power of the leadership of the Holy Spirit is that He will Guide you into all truth and His word can never return void. This means that whatever the Spirit of God speaks to you has to come to pass if you don't quit. You are guaranteed to live undefeated if you listen to the voice of God and are obedient to follow the leadership of His voice. I want to encourage everyone to just talk to God; He Will answer you back and/or give you wisdom from the Scripture. This is very important, because the answer to your life will come from the voice of God's leadership, so never stop listening to the voice of God.

Working Together to Hear God
Brian Head Welch

I hear God in my life in the quiet, in the resting, and in the waiting. What I hear mostly from Him is all these great revelations and encounters with intimacy about who we are together and who He is in me, and who I am in Him. I get awesome revelations, clear words and everything; I have lists of word He's given me. But when it comes to things about location, and business moves and everything, I'm like, I don't get nothing!

It's so encouraging and frustrating, sometimes all together. I talked to a prophet friend of mine, Lou Coulter. And he says he could prophesy to a stick or anybody else, but when it comes to himself, it's just harder for him to hear God's voice for himself. Maybe he makes it that way, but maybe some people can relate to that. So we need a body, and as we work together, we can all hear God in our lives.

To find out more about Brian Welch, visit http://www.brianheadwelch.net/2016/.

Hearing God Through Dreams
Ryan LaStrange

The most common ways I hear the voice of the Lord are as an inner conversation. But there are other ways, and when I think of this, I think of Romans 8:14, which says, "For those who are led by the Spirit of God are the children of God." If we are children of God, we are led by His spirit, and if we are led, we are given communication from the One we are following. Another way God has spoken to me, and probably one of the most life-changing ways, is through prophetic dreams, which I had to learn to interpret. Prophetic dreams are usually in symbols, so you have to pray and seek God to fully understand them. I've also had visions at various times where God has shown me something revealed something to me through the sight realm. I like to journal as well, so many times I get something from the Lord and I write it and come back to pray over it.

Dreams are really interesting and powerful to me, because they are so symbolic. My wife had this dream in which I was on a trip, I was in an accident, and I told her my cheeks had been hurt. When she had the dream, it seemed like just a strange dream, something that made no sense. But later, I realized God was speaking through the dream and it was a warning dream. In the end of the dream, I said to her, "I'm okay."

Well, I went on that trip and something actually happened a few days later. There was an attack against us and against our ministry. And when we looked at the symbolism for cheeks, one of the meanings is accusation. So, immediately, God took us back to the warning dream that I had an accident, said my cheeks were hurt, but I was okay. And it was the voice of the Lord speaking to us: "There's going to be an accusation, but you're going to be okay." And that was exactly what played out. But the way it unfolded, was troubling. And it would have been really, really disheartening and stressful had she not had that prophetic dream.

Regardless, I think we can know if we hear the voice of God or not, because if we hear God, I think we will naturally want to seek and partner with Him.

The first huge encounter I had prophetically, I was sitting in a service in Sacramento, California. I was a newly born again, I was a teenager, and I heard the audible voice of God. One statement from Him shifted my whole life and led me to move, led me to go to Bible college. I got delivered, I got free. I didn't just hear that statement and sit, I heard the statement and immediately started seeking God and asking Him what to do next. So there is a lesson in that when you hear the voice of God, whether it be through a trained audible voice, vision, whatever it is, you have got to then partner that with prayer and continued connection with God.

A big point, though, is that, whether interpreting dreams or learning to hear God's voice in any other way, you've got to give yourself permission to fail. There's got to be trial and error in any life process. And you're going to make mistakes.

I think that too often, people are so afraid of making mistakes that they don't even embark on the journey. As we do this, we can learn what works and what doesn't. I think there are three big ways that can help us identify if we are on the right track or not.

Number one, we know that John 1:1 says, "In the beginning was the Word, and the Word was with God, and the Word was God." So we know that the voice of God is going to be in the Word of God. I've had times where people did things, said things that were very contradictory to the Word. And it was very easy for me to say, you're missing it in this area, it would be easy for me personally, if I had a dream or experienced that, a voice spoke to me, and I couldn't back what that voice was saying to the Word, then I would know.

Another thing is there's typically going to be an inner peace when you hear the voice of God. According to scripture, the prophetic deals with edifying and building up, there's going to be peace. Even when you have a warning dream, there is some sense of peace, because God's voice is in the midst of that one, and He's usually giving instruction. He's cautioning you about something, and letting you know He knows. If I see someone prophesy and there is not peace, I back up and really ask if it is edifying and building people up. If it is not, it is probably not from God.

Thirdly, Revelation teaches us that the prophetic should testify of Jesus. So a real big thing for me when we're dealing with prophetic stuff is it needs to be glorifying and testifying of Jesus. With a lot of people who get into false stuff, their words will be pointing to something else, or someone else besides Jesus.

Finally, mentoring and identity are hugely important when it comes to hearing and speaking God's words. If I was teaching a group that knew nothing about the prophetic, I would now start with teaching about identity, because you're going to be the most powerful and effective when you understand who you are.

As you continue your own journey hearing God, I want to encourage you to be brave. Remember that God wants to talk to you more than you want to hear from Him. He made you! I always say you are hardwired to hear from God. It's like a satellite dish. You were made to receive, capture and release the voice of God. So be brave, and go for it.

For more information on Ryan LeStrange, visit https://www.ryanlestrange.com.

CPSIA information can be obtained
at www.ICGtesting.com
Printed in the USA
FFHW022254150719
53666022-59332FF